BITTEN BY THE BUSINESS BUG
Common Sense Tips for Business and Life
from a Teen Entrepreneur

Jason O'Neill

Pencil Bugs Plus
Temecula, CA
www.pencilbugs.com

Editor: Nancy O'Neill
Cover Design: Chaz DeSimone
www.chazdesimone.com

ISBN-10: 1452862435
ISBN-13: 978-1452862439

First edition – June 2010
Printed by CreateSpace
Printed in the United States of America

*To Mom and Dad
for always loving, supporting, and
encouraging me, no matter what!
Thank you.*

*To Grandpa and Grandma
on the farm for sharing their
wisdom, entrepreneurial
spirit, and hard-working values.*

Contents

Introduction 1
Creating my product 4
Making it legal 9
Give a little 11
Accidental opportunities 13
A little competition 15
You can't get anywhere by sitting on your ideas 18
Getting started in business 21
No one can do it alone 28
Even the smallest things can make a difference 31
You don't have to be tall 37
Customer service 39
Quality vs. quantity 42
A website doesn't guarantee success 44
In the box or out? 47
The importance of networking 55
ROI 58
See the possibilities 61
Learning has no age requirements or restrictions 63
Listen more than you talk 69
Money is funny 72
Spend or save? 75
Public speaking 78
Using notes 84
A little nervousness can be good 87
You can't adlib what you don't know 90
The art of interrupting 92
Admit your mistakes 95
Believe in yourself 98
You are only young once 100
Don't ask a yes or no question 102

Unexpected challenges 105
Everything happens for a reason 107
Expect the unexpected 110
The power of words 113
Don't procrastinate 115
What to do? 117
No guarantees 120
Create your own job 123
Stick to your beliefs 127
Surprise yourself 129
You are not your business 132
Pride doesn't always come naturally 137
Everything in moderation 140
Not like anyone else 143
Everyone can't win 145
Ignore the rules 148
Things are not always what they seem 153
It costs nothing to be polite 160
Offer a solution, not a complaint 162
Three things to make a difference in the world 164
Keeping balanced 167
Textbooks for school – Practical experience and
common sense for life 170
Conclusion 173
What's next? 174
45 tips for business and life 175
About the author 179

INTRODUCTION

Anyone, including kids, can do amazing things but you cannot get anywhere by sitting on your ideas. Regardless of your age, you need to take action. Stop just thinking about it and start doing something. You may surprise yourself. I did!

My name is Jason O'Neill. I am a pretty regular kid. I go to school, do homework, and play with friends. I live with my mom and dad and have a dog named Rusty that we rescued from a shelter. What makes me just a little different from other kids is that I am also an entrepreneur.

If you are already thinking, 'Okay, so he set up a lemonade stand,' you are right. I did. In fact, I set up a few lemonade stands during neighborhood garage sales starting when I was just five years old. Selling lemonade for two summers was really fun. At that age, you do not really think of it as work.

Even though the winters in southern California are warmer than a lot of other places and people still hold garage sales, lemonade just does not sell when it is fifty degrees. I liked hot chocolate in the winter and I figured that a lot of other people probably did too. When I was eight years old, I started my third business. I set up a stand selling hot chocolate in our driveway. It seemed a little weird to me that people were having garage sales right before Christmas but that gave me another idea besides just offering hot chocolate. I took out some of my favorite Christmas CDs, found a Santa stocking cap that fit, and out I went to drum up business as people drove by toward other houses with garage sales. I sang Christmas carols, danced a little, waved a lot, and yelled "Merry Christmas" when cars passed by. Surprisingly, I sold a lot of hot chocolate in just a couple of hours. At fifty cents a cup – no extra charge for marshmallows – I raked in about thirty dollars. Unlike when I had my lemonade stands, this time my parents made me pay for the supplies to teach me about the cost of doing business, gross sales, and net profits. A lot of kids I knew thought that whatever money they took in was what they actually made. I learned very quickly that there is a big difference between gross and net.

By the time I was nine, my fourth business was giving me a small, but steady monthly income. I made up fliers and delivered them to our neighbors letting them know that I was starting a recycling business. All people had to do to help the environment, and me, was to toss their plastic bottles and aluminum cans in a bag and I would pick them up on a regular basis with my mom or dad. I did not even require that people sort or wash the cans and bottles which I later realized was not such a good idea. Some people left soda and other sticky liquids in containers so when I would get the bags home, I had to dump everything on the lawn and spray it with the hose. My recycling business was all profit. Free money. I did not have any supplies to buy, no products to make, and my parents did not even make me pay for the gas it took to drive to the recycling center. I was doing pretty well until I lost my first customer. It never occurred to me that people might move out of the neighborhood but that is just what happened. The first customer to sign up with me was also the first to leave. After that, I realized that there was always a chance that I could lose other customers for one reason or another. Before I lost any more customers, I decided to pass out more fliers in another neighborhood nearby but still within walking distance. That business taught me a good lesson. Customers will come and go so you always need to work on expanding your customer base.

When I started my first few businesses, I never really thought about being an entrepreneur at that point. In fact, at that age, I wasn't even sure what entrepreneur meant.

Becoming an entrepreneur with a successful product business happened by accident right before my tenth birthday. This is where the story begins.

CREATING MY PRODUCT

My mom was painting some wooden door-stoppers to sell at a craft fair before Thanksgiving. I had a brilliant idea. At least I was convinced it was brilliant. I made her a deal. "Mom, if I help you paint your doorstoppers, will you split the money you make with me?"

"No deal," said Mom. "If you want to sell something and make money, you will have to come up with your own idea."

While that might stop some kids, it did not stop me. I started drawing out designs for possible products I could make. I knew I had to keep it simple but wanted to make something for kids.

My first idea was to paint faces on wooden clothes pins. I was not sure what they would be good for but they were kind of cute. Mom and Dad suggested something a little more useful. As I was drawing out more designs, I looked at the pencil I was using.

"I've got it!" I shouted. "I'll make something to put on top of a pencil."

Original? Not really. I knew that there were all kinds of pencil toppers already sold in stores. I had collected plenty of my own since I started school but I was determined to make my pencil toppers different from the rest. For starters, they would be made by a kid which later became part of my slogan, *Made by a kid but not just for kids!* Mine would also be removable so that kids could still use the eraser. So many other pencil toppers were permanently glued to the pencil. Later on, I created a Certificate of Authenticity for each

Pencil Bug which was a little story that included their birth date, given name, and care and training instructions. But at the time I first had the idea, all I was thinking about was making a couple of dozen for the craft fair so originality was not a big factor. I continued with my idea.

I have always liked school and for the most part, I did not mind homework but I knew not all kids were like me. Having a cute, original pencil topper just might make doing homework a little more fun for some kids.

After several more designs on paper and asking Mom's advice on different materials we could easily buy at local craft stores, Pencil Bugs were coming to life.

Let me stop here for a minute. At that time, the product name I had initially chosen was Pencil Pals. It was cute, catchy, and easy to say. I will tell you later why I eventually had to change the name. Now back to the story.

Using ten dollars of my own money for the initial supplies, I bought everything I needed to make a couple of dozen Pencil Pals. I started out with one-inch white Styrofoam balls that we hand painted in eight different colors. Next came two googley eyes and two small wire antennas that we glued on. In the beginning, we could not find a pre-made spiral object to use as an antenna. We bought craft wire and cut it into two-inch pieces which Mom then wound around a nail into a spiral pattern. Each one was always different since there was no way to wind them exactly the same. It was very time-consuming and hard on her fingers. None of us thought much about the difficult parts since

I was only planning on making enough for the one craft fair. After the eyes and antennas were secure, we punched a hole in the ball, hot-glued in a black fuzzy pipe cleaner, set the head on top of a standard #2 pencil and wrapped the pipe cleaner around the pencil about a third of the way down. The finished Pencil Pal hugged the pencil nicely. Before long, we had twenty-four done and ready to sell.

The craft fair was in North Dakota where my grandma lives so we shipped my products and Mom's doorstoppers to Grandma. It was a pretty good deal for me. I did not have to pay for any of the shipping or the table rental at the fair. And since we could not go there personally, Grandma even sold them for me but I still got all the profits.

When the craft fair was over and we got a call from Grandma, I was really surprised. Pencil Pals jumped off the table quickly. They were a big hit. It seemed that everyone wanted one for themselves, their kids, or their grandkids. In fact, all twenty-four of them sold out. When I heard the news, I wished that I would have made more to send but who knew that they would be so popular? Mom was not so lucky with her doorstoppers. Only two of them were purchased.

I was happy. Really happy! I made money and people liked my product. I stashed my money away and did not give it too much thought after that.

During Christmas break, Mom suggested that I make a few more just for fun since I still had some supplies left. I took a couple of Pencil Pals to school. Kids used all kinds of different pencils with toppers and weird erasers so I never really gave it much thought when I put a Pencil Pal on my own pencil and started writing. But kids noticed right away because it was different. They wanted to know where I had bought it. The buzz about Pencil Pals travelled fast. Before I knew it, I was taking orders for specific colors and making more money.

It still had not occurred to me that this would become a real business. I was just having fun making things other kids really wanted. Without realizing it then, I was becoming an entrepreneur in fourth grade. As more kids found out about my little business, some followed my example. One girl in my class made and sold miniature clay figurines but that did not last long. Most of the other kids only *talked* about doing something. Apparently, this is common for people of all ages.

I never felt I was an inspiration to other people but looking back, I am glad I had a positive effect on at least a few kids in grade school.

While one girl tried her own business, others wanted in on *my* action. They volunteered to advertise and sell for me, which was great since all I had to do was give them a free Pencil Pal in return. I did not have a marketing budget and I could not afford to pay salespeople. I was learning that you can still do a lot of advertising and sales without any budget at all. You just have to be more creative.

Other kids offered to help me make my products. I had to turn them down. Pencil Pals were not easy to make and I was very particular about their quality. I never felt anyone could do it as well as I could.

A very important point. When I say "I", it is important to know that my business has never been a one-man job. Without a ton of help and support from my parents, I would not have been able to get this far and you would not be reading this book right now.

The best, but most surprising, offer I received was from a classmate in fourth grade. One boy wanted to buy my business. He pulled out two fifty dollar bills he had in his pocket. I wondered why a fourth grader had that much money at school in the first place but that wasn't the point. For whatever reason he did not want to start his own business, he offered to buy mine. I figured that it was because he thought it would be easier since I already had everything in place: the product, how to make it, and customers.

Most kids would have accepted his offer but not me. Even though I was only charging fifty cents per Pencil Pal at that time (the discounted price for kids at my school), I knew I was going to make more than his hundred dollars with my business.

That is when it really hit me. If another kid wanted to buy my business, I knew I had something good going.

MAKING IT LEGAL

I had big plans so I needed to make everything legal. This is when I changed my product name from Pencil Pals to Pencil Bugs. My mom was looking up possible domain names for my website and found that Pencil Pals was already taken. After some discussion, I decided on Pencil Bugs. It was still cute and the name was available. So Pencil Bugs it was. Since I had been selling my products at school for a couple of months by that time, it took a little while to get kids used to the new name but that was a small detail.

Since minors cannot sign any legal documents, my parents applied for a business license for me, a DBA (my "doing business as" name), and a sales tax ID. I designed my logo and business cards. My mom created my website and set up a PayPal account. I was ready for business - real business.

Deciding on my DBA was an interesting experience. I wanted the words Pencil Bugs in part of the name but I knew that my business name should be different from my product name, even if it was just slightly different. Normally the company name is not the same as the product name. And what if I came up with other products? What if I had more than just Pencil Bugs? How would that affect my business name? After some brainstorming, we decided on Pencil Bugs Plus. It was easily identifiable with the product name but it still gave me the flexibility of expanding in pretty much any direction with related products.

BIZ TIP: Don't pick the first business or product name you think of. Give it a lot of thought. It will be harder and more costly later on to change your mind.

GIVE A LITTLE

Before long, I was making some decent money. I had always been good about saving money from birthday and Christmas gifts and my small recycling business but I really did not have a way to continue earning more money until Pencil Bugs were born. I was not getting rich but I had more money than most kids my age and I was earning it.

One night, we were having a family discussion over dinner. Somehow the subject of orphanages came up. I did not even know what an orphanage was until Mom explained it. She said there are not many orphanages left and that most kids are placed in foster care with other families if they cannot stay at home. We talked more about how foster agencies worked. Even though foster homes sounded much better than orphanages, I could only imagine how hard it would be to live with someone else. I was lucky and very thankful. I had two parents living in the same house. Dad had a good job and Mom was able to stay home to take care of me. Yep, I was lucky but I realized not all kids were.

I asked my parents how charities worked.

"It's good to donate to help others but you have to be careful," they said. "Some are not so honest and the money you give may not always get to those who really need it."

I did not like the sound of that. I was not going to pay for people's salaries. My money had to go straight to help kids.

Starting with kids in my own community made the most sense. After looking around a bit, we found a local foster agency in town that agreed to use one hundred percent of my donations for the foster kids. Each quarter when I took my donation check to them, they would ask what I wanted them to buy for the kids. If it was close to Christmas, I always suggested toys, clothes, or blankets for babies. Before school started, I asked that they buy school supplies which every kid needs. It made me feel good to know that I was helping in my own way.

ACCIDENTAL OPPORTUNITIES

That is how it all started. From a simple creation to sell at a craft fair to a successful business, Pencil Bugs have given me more opportunities than I could have ever imagined. I have learned so many things about business and life that schools never teach kids. One of the best parts about having my business is that I am able to speak at schools, organizations, and events encouraging kids to try their own ideas. It has been so much fun sharing my story.

I am not going to lie to you though. There have also been plenty of times that I have wanted to quit. Sometimes it is hard, really hard. My parents have always encouraged me to keep going. I guess they could see the long-term potential and benefits for me. It is hard for a kid to think that far ahead sometimes. I am glad they did not let me give up. Everyone, especially a kid, needs a little push now and then. It is okay to get discouraged and want to quit. Don't be too hard on yourself for feeling that way. It is normal.

Because I wanted to save as much of my money as possible, we were always looking for new marketing options without spending any money. With my mom's help, I set up a blog. It went live on November 2, 2008 - my thirteenth birthday. I was not exactly sure what I would write about or how often I would have time to post since school comes first, but everyone kept telling me I needed to add a blog for more exposure.

Then in early December, I started a Twitter account. One more online thing to keep up with but I thought I would give it a try. That was one of the best no-cost marketing decisions I ever made. I received so much exposure and made some very good friends that have continued to be supportive and inspirational.

As more people started following what I was doing with my business, I was also reading tips from other entrepreneurs. If other people could share their business tips, then why couldn't I? Age does not matter when it comes to learning. Even the youngest person can teach and inspire others.

Twelve days before Christmas, I posted my first BizTip on Twitter. The tweet was simple. It said:

> *12 BizTips of Christmas – Day 1* "Help *someone because even the smallest thing can make a difference.*"

Positive comments poured in. It was amazing. BizTips for Days 2-12 followed with a business-related story posted on my blog each day. By Christmas, the idea of writing my own business book came to life.

I have had a lot of amazing experiences and opportunities, thanks to all the people who have supported me and shared their knowledge, especially my parents. They have taught me lessons that I have applied to business but also to life in general. Much of what I have learned and share in this book is really just common sense but sometimes it takes a kid to simplify things.

A LITTLE COMPETITION

My first lemonade stand was fun. Well, almost everything is fun at five years old. It was so much fun that I decided to set up another one the next summer. I was expecting pretty much the same arrangement. Mom would help me make the lemonade, buy the paper cups, get the change bag ready, and set up the table. All I would have to do is sit by my table and wait for people to walk or drive by. I had no idea that I would learn about competition at six years old.

As we planned how much lemonade and other supplies to buy in the days before, Mom suggested that we make cookies to sell also. That sounded like a good idea to me. I decided that most people liked chocolate chip so she added the necessary ingredients to the shopping list.

The day before, she was busy making cookies. After they cooled, I helped her wrap each one in plastic so they looked just like the ones in the store. Normally when she baked cookies, they were average size. For my lemonade sale, and now cookies too, I asked her if she could make them jumbo size. I was selling my lemonade for fifty cents and thought that if the cookies were big enough, I could ask fifty cents per cookie too.

She agreed and the cookies turned out perfectly. We made a few dozen that were all neatly wrapped. Well, maybe not all of them were so neatly wrapped. After all, I was only six years old so I am sure my wrapping skills were not the best.

Everything was ready. Early Saturday morning, we hauled out my toy cash register stand and table and chair to the edge of the driveway, leaned the homemade sign against the table and I was open for business. The weather was warm. People were driving and walking by looking for the next house in the neighborhood that had a garage sale. As they passed our house, I would say "hi." They would smile and say "hi" back but people were not stopping to buy. I could not figure it out. The summer before, I had sold a lot of lemonade. This time I had homemade cookies too. Why weren't people stopping to buy?

I was tired of sitting and not selling very much so Dad suggested I take a walk with him around the neighborhood to see which houses were holding garage sales. Our neighborhood had one street into the area. Right at the entrance, we discovered another boy with a lemonade stand of his own. We walked closer to check it out. He was not selling lemonade at all. He had store-bought juice boxes and store-bought candy and was reselling those. Mine was all homemade. Why were people lined up at his house and not at mine? It did not make any sense.

"Jason, where is his house?" Dad asked.

Couldn't Dad see his house? We were standing right in front of it.

"Right here," I said pointing at the boy's house.

Dad laughed but then explained that because that boy's house was right at the entrance of the neighborhood and ours was a couple of streets in, he was getting the people first.

"What can we do about it?" I asked. "I want people to buy my stuff instead of his."

I do not remember what Dad said exactly but looking back on that now and learning so much more about business since then, there were a lot of things that we could have done. I would have made up another sign and posted it right near the entrance so as people drove in, they would have seen that there was a lemonade and cookie stand just two streets over. As people passed by our house, I could also have done more to get their attention.

BIZ TIP: Looking back is easy. Making changes today is what matters.

Learning about competition at six years old was hard. I guess life lessons are not supposed to be easy. By the next summer, we had moved from that neighborhood so I never got the chance to try out my other ideas.

YOU CAN'T GET ANYWHERE BY SITTING ON YOUR IDEAS

Think of how many times you have heard someone say things like, "I thought of that product years ago," or "Hey, that was my idea," or "I could have invented that."

People make these types of statements pretty often. You might be one of those people who said something similar when you saw a product sitting on the store shelf or advertised on TV. Maybe you actually did come up with the same concept before that other guy's product hit the market. The difference was, that guy did something about his idea. You didn't. But it does not have to be that way. YOU could be the one that other people are saying that about. It could be YOUR idea that makes it onto the store shelves.

When I speak at events, one of the things I always mention is that an idea does not have to be brain surgery or rocket science. It can be the simplest thing in the world.

BIZ TIP: An idea is just a thought unless you act on it.

Pencil Bugs did not require an engineer to design them. I did not need any special training or equipment to get started. There certainly are dozens of choices of pencil toppers for kids but still, I have become pretty successful with my simple idea.

There are a lot of reasons why some people never actually put their ideas into motion but if you do not at least give it a try, how will you ever know what might have happened? YOU could have the next big idea.

My mom is a classic example of someone not taking the next step. When she and her sisters were little, they came up with a game idea. It was a simple concept they thought of while playing with the vacuum cleaner hose. Sounds silly already, right? That is what I thought at first too. Apparently living on a farm in the middle of North Dakota, kids got bored so they often made up their own games.

Most of the vacuums back then were canister types. A single hose attached to one end for vacuuming but you could also attach the hose to a hole on the other end of the canister which would then blow air out instead.

When the vacuum hose was attached to the blower end, Mom and her sisters realized it was powerful enough to keep a ping pong ball suspended in mid air. Once the ball was in the air, if they tilted the hose too far over to the side, naturally the ball would drop to the floor. The object of their homemade game was to see who could keep the ball in the air the longest. When that became too easy, it was a challenge to see who could keep the ball floating while tilting the hose down the farthest. Pretty simple, right? No cost involved. No batteries to worry about. Always available anytime they wanted to play their new game.

Mom said they talked with their parents about trying to get it manufactured but they just did not have the money or the time to do anything about it. Since Internet had not been invented yet, finding the resources would have been much harder too. Like most people with ideas, it was not too long until they forgot all about their fun invention. That was, until they saw a TV commercial for a brand new game with the same concept. Of course it did not involve a real vacuum cleaner but it had a blower unit with lightweight balls included. The object of the game was basically the same.

When one of Mom's sisters saw the game on TV, she shouted what most people would, "Hey, there's our game!" That was about all they could do except for bragging rights within their own family.

The first time I heard Mom tell that story, I asked if the game is still sold today. "No," she said but she could not remember how successful it actually was or how long it lasted in the stores.

Money, time, and access to available resources are big factors when trying to get your ideas off the drawing board. That is why if you can, keep it simple in the beginning. Look around you. Sometimes the silliest ideas make the best products. How many times have you seen a product that has no function? It is just cute. Remember the pet rock? Of course, that was long before I was even born but the fact that its creator made over a million dollars on something that useless from a simple idea really fascinated me when I heard about it.

Functional products usually solve problems. Some products are created by accident. Others are just for fun or for decoration. Whatever your idea is, take action.

LIFE TIP: Doing nothing will guarantee nothing.

GETTING STARTED IN BUSINESS

So you want to become an entrepreneur. Maybe you are tired of depending on someone else for your income. Maybe you want to be more creative than your regular job allows you to be. Maybe you want to spend more time with your kids. Or maybe you are still in school and think that this is the best time to give it a try. Whatever the reason is, you need to take the first step. Just thinking about it will not get you anywhere.

Starting a business does not have to be complicated, especially in the beginning. Too many people do not even try because they feel that there is too much to do or they do not have the skills or knowledge it takes. Some people are not even sure about what product or service they want to offer.

If you are having a hard time coming up with an idea, get some people together to brainstorm. When I created Pencil Bugs, it started with a desire to make money and a simple brainstorming session one afternoon. It did not take very long before I decided how I wanted my product to look, what it would be made of, and how to assemble it. Family and friends are good sources for getting ideas. Just remember, talk with people you trust and be cautious. Otherwise, you could be one of those unfortunate stories where someone else ran with your idea and you ended up with nothing.

BIZ TIP: From the moment you get an idea, start keeping a journal.

Make sure that your journal has a permanent binding where pages cannot be added. Do not use a three-ring binder with loose paper. Write down every idea you have and everything you do relating to your business. Keep it organized in chronological order and as complete as possible. You may need to use this journal later on to help prove that you had the idea before someone else did.

Not every suggestion I offer will pertain to every type of business or individual. Many tips can be applied to business in general but since Pencil Bugs is product-based, much of the information I have learned specifically relates to product businesses. The following are some basic questions to ask before you jump in with both feet.

Why do people need your product or service? Are there any other similar products or services already available? If there are, what makes yours unique so that a customer would want to buy or use yours over an existing one? Where would you sell the product? Who would your customers be and what is their age range? Basically, you need to understand the competition in order for you to assess your own product. Many businesses fail because they do not do their homework.

In order to start any business, you need money even if it is a small amount. However, it is not necessary to take out huge loans or get investors. Evaluate your financial situation. Figure out the minimum amount that you will need to get started and try to work within that budget. It is not impossible and there is no need to overspend. Working on a budget just means you need to find more creative ways to manage your money. It can be done though. I started with just ten dollars. Starting out small is one of the biggest advantages a young entrepreneur has. We can afford to take our time and not rush into things. Regardless of how old you are when you become an entrepreneur or what type of business you start, you can still start out small and look for investors or other sources of capital when you are ready to expand.

Calculate how much your product costs to make before you decide how much to sell it for. This may be obvious to most adults but I have met many kids who wanted to start their own business after seeing what I had done. The part they overlooked was the cost of supplies because their parents paid for those. Most kids did not realize that you have to calculate the cost of materials into the whole equation and that there is a huge difference between gross sales and net profits.

Once you have done your initial homework, make a small quantity and test out your product. Try selling your product to friends, neighbors, or at school to find out if people are willing to buy it. There is no need to approach retail stores right away or even set up a website until you are sure your product is marketable.

Note: If you are a student and want to test market at your school, make sure you check with the principal to get permission first.

Deciding what your sale price will be can be tricky. If you start out too high, customers may not want to buy it. If you start out too low, it can be hard to raise your price later on once people are used to the original price. From the craft fair and through the first couple of months in business, I tested out several different prices to see what people were willing to pay. When I first sold Pencil Bugs to kids at school, I gave them a huge discount in order to increase how many I sold. I was willing to sell more at a lower price to get more people buzzing about Pencil Bugs. Once I got my business license and tax ID and started selling officially through my website and at other events in my community, I raised the price but still not too much. A few months later, I received a very important piece of advice from an owner of a large company.

"If you set your price too low," he said, "people will think you have a cheap [poorly made] product. People often associate quality with price. If you don't think your product is worth more, then you should not be making or selling it."

He was right. Be confident in your product. Offer quality at a fair price but do not undervalue yourself or your product. When those factors are considered, customers will buy.

Not everyone, adults and children alike, has the same financial knowledge or experience. Regardless of your age, many people need help with the financial part of business. If you pretend to know everything or are afraid to ask for help, you could run into bigger problems later on.

Many start-up companies that take big risks in the beginning or expand too fast often go out of business. There are no guarantees. I have heard people say they have risked everything they own to start a business or get their product manufactured.

My grandpa was born in 1924. He has a lot of years of experience behind him and is full of good common sense advice. "Don't loan money unless you are willing to never get it back," Grandpa says. The same advice goes for taking big risks in business with your own money. If it does not work and you have spent everything you have, what will you do if your business fails? One of the most important things to remember in any situation is to have a Plan B. Try to think of the "what if's" so you are not surprised and end up with nothing. Having alternate plans will not guarantee that your business will be successful but at least you will be better prepared.

You are making progress. Your brainstorming is done. You have your idea. You have perfected your prototype. You have researched comparable products. You know who your customers will be. You have done a test market. You are ready to start production. The next question is, "Who should manufacture it?" My suggestion is to do it yourself if at all possible. Most home-based businesses start out that way. Many entrepreneurs are putting their heart and soul into making their products right in their kitchens, spare bedrooms, garages, or basements.

Keeping production at home will help keep initial expenses down. On the flip side, your house may turn into something you do not recognize. Until a manufacturing deal is made to mass produce Pencil Bugs, my production line takes place on our large kitchen island. However, since I made my first products, we have streamlined the production process quite a bit. With the help of my parents, we now limit production to weekends only and make large quantities at a time, building up the inventory on a regular basis. This means we can actually use our kitchen for cooking and eating as normal.

There are so many home-based businesses run by kids even younger than I am, all with the help of their parents and sometimes the entire family. Since I started using social networking sites like Twitter and Facebook, I have also met many, many stay-at-home moms who chose that option because it gave them the freedom and flexibility to spend more time with their kids.

I never realized all of the benefits that people can have with home businesses until I started mine. My parents and I have always spent a lot of time together but starting Pencil Bugs gave us a whole new perspective. There have been fun times but also many difficult ones. Somehow you learn to work through the tough times. It also gives you one more goal that you all have in common.

If a parent is starting the business, try involving your kids even on a small scale. It teaches kids about finance, sales, and marketing among many other skills that they will not learn in school. If the child is the one with the entrepreneurial spirit, parents should support them as much as possible. No one can do it alone, especially kids. Minors will need a parent's help with legal aspects. No matter who actually starts the business or whose idea it is, starting a business can be a lot of fun for the whole family.

Making your first products for sale will be exciting. How many you make initially depends on a lot of factors and only you can answer that. When I first made Pencil Bugs, I only made two dozen since my initial purpose was to sell at the one craft fair. I bought supplies from local retail stores even though I realized later on that my initial cost per unit was much more expensive because of that. As my business continued to grow, I bought supplies in bulk.

LIFE TIP: Be patient. Don't give up!

There will be times when you want to quit. I have had my share for sure. It takes a lot of hard work but it can be worth it in the long run. My business has not made millions yet but the opportunities and experiences I have had are priceless.

So go for it! Give it a try. You might be surprised at what you can do. If you just keep taking small steps, one at a time, something big will eventually happen. All you need is an idea and the will to do it.

BIZ TIP: You have to make things happen but don't force things to happen.

NO ONE CAN DO IT ALONE

Being a kid and having a business can be really fun but it also means that you are going to need a lot of help from adults. That does not necessarily mean it has to be a parent's help. I am thankful that mine support me but let's face it, some parents just do not have the time or are not equipped to be a support person or mentor for one reason or another.

LIFE TIP: It is okay to ask for help.

If you are determined, you can find mentors in many different places. A teacher or school counselor might help, although from my experience, not many traditional teachers are entrepreneurial minded. But you might be lucky and have just the right person at your school. A mentor could also be a friend's parent or even an older brother or sister. If you belong to a church or community organization like Boy or Girl Scouts, those could also be good resources. Junior Achievement is a global organization and has branch offices in most major areas. They teach kids business skills and provide entrepreneurial assistance through the schools. You can even find resources online.

The point is, you are going to need help. Even if you are an adult starting a business, no one can do it alone. You may think you can but chances are, there is always at least one thing you will have to learn from someone else or get help with.

In fact, whenever I hear someone say that they run their whole business without any help, I do not believe them.

There are also people who have the philosophy, "Ask forgiveness, not permission." That seems a little backward. If you have to worry about someone not supporting your ideas and efforts to where you just go ahead and plan on saying "sorry" after the fact, then you probably do not have the right people supporting or believing in you. Find someone else.

Setting up my business legally required a lot of help from my parents. Did I know anything about all of the legal aspects that were involved? Of course not. I was only in the fourth grade. Could I have researched all of the information myself online? Maybe, if I actually knew what I was looking for in the first place. Even if I had found all the answers, I would not have been able to sign anything legal.

My mom called about getting a business license and told them it was for her ten-year-old son's business. The woman on the phone asked all kinds of questions to determine what I was doing, how much time I was spending on my business and a lot of other questions. Being the curious Mom that she is, after about the fourth or fifth question, she asked why it mattered how much time I spent on my business. It turned out that they wanted to make sure that I was not being used as unfair child labor. When Mom hung up, we all laughed because I was a normal kid with homework and still had a lot of time to play. Business never comes first and I do not believe it should for any kid. You still need time to be a normal kid. And if you are lucky enough to have supportive parents, they will help you stay balanced.

Regardless of your age, if you decide to become an entrepreneur, it is good to learn as much about all aspects of business as possible. That does not mean you end up doing everything yourself. But if you at least understand the various parts, there is less chance that someone could take advantage of you.

I do not worry about that right now because my business only involves my family. I do my own bank statements and deposits and have Mom double check them just to make sure. I know exactly how much I have. If the time ever comes where Mom and I are not doing the accounting ourselves, at least I can double check the other person's work if necessary. I have heard stories where someone takes off with all of the money from a business and the owner does not even realize until it is too late.

You cannot do it alone. Be smart. Get reliable help and support when and where you need it. As a biz kid, you will need it especially to get started. Just continue to learn as much as you can.

EVEN THE SMALLEST THINGS CAN MAKE A DIFFERENCE

It is not always about the money. I often get asked how much my business is worth or how many Pencil Bugs I have sold or how much I have made. For me, money has not been my main focus.

BIZ TIP: Money is good to have but it is more important what you do with it once you have it.

There are so many people that need help from others and there are just as many different ways that a person can donate or volunteer.

Knowing how charities work is very important. One day I hope to be like Warren Buffett or Bill Gates so that I can support major organizations and causes. In the meantime, I know that what I am doing is still appreciated.

Everyone has something to give. It does not have to be thousands or even hundreds of dollars. It does not even have to be material gifts. There are many other ways a person can help. Even though it is hard to find extra time, it is one of the most valuable contributions a person can make. Sometimes I get really busy with school and homework. It takes effort to find extra time to volunteer. But then I remember people who are less fortunate and doing something to help others can make a big difference in someone else's life.

After donating money to the foster agency for the first two years of my business, I wanted to find another way to help other kids.

Other than a trip to the emergency room for a playground accident in first grade, the only time I have been in the hospital was when I was born. I can only imagine what it must be like to be in a hospital for other reasons, especially for a child. I know if I had to be in the hospital for an illness, I would want things to do to get my mind off the reason why I was there in the first place.

We found the closest, biggest children's hospital and contacted them about donations. Rady Children's Hospital in San Diego, California is part of the Children's Miracle Network. It turned out that since we did not have a children's hospital in our town, any kids that needed serious care had to drive about an hour to that hospital. By choosing Rady Children's Hospital, I was actually helping kids from my own community too. After talking with the hospital donation coordinator, the best way I could help was to set up a gift bag program.

Every quarter, I use part of my proceeds to buy toys, games, books, and other activities for the kids. I also donate my Pencil Bugs products.

I have delivered dozens of gift bags to the hospital. After my first delivery, I realized that once the hospital staff had given out the gift bags, there would be more kids admitted to the hospital before my next donation. We learned that they had a community playroom with larger toys and games that the kids and families could check out to take to their room or use in the playroom. From that point on, in addition to the individual toys, I started buying board games, activity sets, DVDs, video games, and anything else that I found in stores that I would like to have access to if I were in the hospital.

I was not spending a lot of money but I was still able to buy a lot of gifts. If you learn how to bargain shop, your money can go a long way. We watched the store ads for sales and found really good deals. People forget that they can do a lot on a small budget if they plan it carefully.

I have always been the type of kid that would rather save my money than spend it but knowing I was spending money to benefit other kids was actually pretty fun. At the end of each quarter once we calculated how much money I had to spend, we would hit the toy stores and any other places that had good sales going on. Filling up a shopping cart to the top with all kinds of toys and games was not as easy as it sounds because I always tried to get the most for my money. I took my time and comparison shopped, just like Mom does. By the time I was done, I knew that I had bought the most I could within my budget. Pushing a cart full of toys around the store made me feel a little weird and almost guilty at times as people starred, probably wondering what one kid could do with all of those toys. If a person looked long enough, I would usually volunteer that I was buying everything to donate to a children's hospital. Once they heard that, they were very supportive and encouraging.

Shopping was easy compared to the effort it took to organize the toys and put together the gift bags. My donation before Christmas 2008 was a challenge. I wanted to make it extra special for the kids so I put a request on my website asking for additional donations of toys, books, and any other products that people might want to donate. My hope was to have enough goodies to fill fifty bags. Fourteen small business owners responded with a wide variety of products and money donations.

Mom, Dad, and I got busy and set out all of the bags in our game room, lined up in neat rows ready to fill with toys. None of us realized just how much space fifty canvas shopping bags would take up. We took the time to separate the boys' and girls' toys, categorize by age, and then label each bag. I also wrote and signed a letter to include in each bag so that the kids knew another kid was thinking about them.

Whew! That was a bigger job than I expected. Then came the real surprise. How were we going to get all of the bags into Dad's car to deliver them to the hospital? None of us had thought about that small detail. In addition to the fifty individual bags, we also had larger bags with big items like board games, musical toys, and balls. There was no way everything would fit into a Toyota Camry. Even if Mom and Dad drove both of their cars, everything still was not going to fit.

"Why not get a rental car company to donate a van?" I suggested. "If we tell them that I am delivering toys to kids in the hospital, maybe they would help out."

A few calls later and Mom found one company that was willing to give us a fifty percent discount but that was the best they could do. I was happy with that. Half off was better than no van at all. We made a quick trip to pick up the van and then back to the house to load all of the toys. They barely fit in the van. We used every available inch in the back as well as on the seat next to me and also the floor. You could see red canvas bags piled high from every window. I wanted Dad to wear a Santa hat but he said no. So I did. What a trip that was!

Christmas 2009 had to be even bigger and better. I got to work in July on a fundraiser. My goal was to raise enough money to buy 250 teddy bears for the kids at Rady Children's Hospital. I was going to include my own money too but I still had no idea if I would meet my goal or not.

By the beginning of November, I had raised enough money to buy about 400 teddy bears. I was pretty happy but I still had about a month to go. The week before Thanksgiving, the local NBC station in San Diego interviewed me for the four o'clock news. The very next day, my story was picked up by MSN and hit their home page online. Donations poured in from all over the world. From a boy in Alaska with a $5 donation to a company in New York making a $500 donation, every dollar mattered.

I appreciated each donation but there were a few that really surprised me. One day I received an email from a group of eighth grade students in Michigan. They had held a bake sale and were planning on donating the money to a local hospital. For some reason, they ran out of time so they found my fundraiser online. Since I was doing something similar, they decided to donate the $119 they had raised from the bake sale to support my teddy bear fundraiser.

Another surprise donation was from three military guys stationed in Iraq. Not only did they donate $150 but one of them sent an email telling me how proud they were of me for helping kids here while they were over there fighting to keep us safe here. Getting that email meant a lot to me.

By my deadline in mid-December, I had raised $5,130 which enabled me to buy 1800 teddy bears. I also received a special donation of a dozen assorted stuffed animals from the Build-A-Bear Workshop and several teddy bears from the Junior Achievement organization.

It was a huge success. I continue to receive emails from parents whose child received one of my teddy bears, thanking me for my generosity.

Whatever you decide to do in life, whether you start your own business or work for someone else, think about ways you can help others. Even if it is in a small way, it still matters.

You Don't Have To Be Tall

My very first school presentation was to a first grade class at my elementary school. Their teacher had talked a lot about me in the days before. The buzz about Pencil Bugs had spread through the school so several of the kids already had their very own Pencil Bug. By the time my big day came, it was exciting for everyone.

I was only in the fourth grade so I did not feel I was that much older than the first graders. I also was not that much taller than many of them.

As I walked up to the classroom door, I peeked through the window and saw all of the kids sitting criss-cross apple sauce in a big group on the floor in one corner of the room.

Butterflies flew around in my stomach until the teacher opened the door. I heard whispers and giggles from the kids.

"Shhh, be quiet children," the teacher instructed her class as she invited me in.

One little girl nudged her friend sitting beside her. "He's here!" she squealed, pointing at the door.

I turned around to see what famous person was behind me. I was sure she could not have been referring to me. No one was there except my mom, carrying a small box of Pencil Bugs, her purse, and the video camera. They were excited about me. What a surprise!

The presentation went very well. I talked for about fifteen minutes to leave time for questions. By the time I was a big fourth grader, I had forgotten how curious little kids could be.

I answered question after question, sometimes answering the same one from multiple students. I could tell by the looks on their faces that they were fascinated. It was a good feeling to know that I made an impression on them.

In addition to giving talks to schools, I have also spoken to many adult audiences. Oddly enough, I often get the same reactions from them as I do from little kids.

Regardless of what age the audience is or who I talk with one-on-one, people tell me that I am someone to admire which always makes me feel good.

I recognize that at my age, I have only just begun. However, you don't have to be tall for people to look up to you.

Being a role model comes with a lot of responsibility. I try to keep things in perspective, enjoy my business and the opportunities it has given me while still having fun being a regular kid.

CUSTOMER SERVICE

Many older people can probably remember when a company's philosophy was "the customer is always right." Customers were treated with respect. Employees were trained to do everything they could to keep the customers happy. I can imagine that was probably hard to do because some customers can be pretty difficult at times. Luckily, I have not experienced many difficult customers with my business.

Even if the customer isn't always right, businesses would not exist without customers. My business is still relatively small so I am able to send a personal thank you and confirmation for every order I receive through my website. If someone just wants to ask me a question, I always send a reply back.

LIFE TIP: Treat people with respect because every person matters.

Learning to give good customer service, no matter what type of business you have, will help keep your business going. There are so many options and products available that it is pretty easy for people to shop other places if they are not satisfied.

Word of mouth advertising can travel fast. Bad press travels even faster. Once you lose customers or make them unhappy, you will have to work twice as hard to earn their business back.

It is the same as trusting someone. If a person does something that makes you distrust them, it takes a lot more effort on their part to gain your trust again. It is much easier to do things right in the first place.

Regardless if your business is big or small, sometimes the littlest things make all the difference in the world.

No one wants unhappy customers but in the event that a customer becomes dissatisfied, keep your eyes and ears open. You can learn a lot from their feedback.

Customer service has been a top priority with me. This has been my daily checklist since the day I officially started Pencil Bugs.

- Check my email every day.
- Reply within 24-48 hours. Even if I do not have an immediate answer, at least I let them know I received their email and I am working on it.
- With every order I receive through my website, I send a personal thank you email letting the customer know I received their order and when it will be shipped.
- If someone sends an email just with a comment, I respond to those also. If they took the time to write to me, I take the time to acknowledge them.

These may be obvious, simple things but just think how often you leave a message for someone or send an email and never hear back from them. How does it make you feel? Without any response, people start assuming whatever they want and many times, it is not positive.

BIZ TIP: Without customers, you have no business.

People have asked me if I plan on giving the same kind of customer service as my business grows. It is hard to say how things will change. In order to run a huge business successfully in the future, I know that I will need many people to do various jobs. I will not be the one who is sitting taking orders or dealing with customers directly like I do now but the customer will always come first because without them, Pencil Bugs would not exist.

QUALITY VS. QUANTITY

Even at my age, I see things that make me wonder about quality versus quantity. I think sometimes people focus on how much money they can make instead of being concerned about the quality of their products. I did not start my business thinking I was going to get rich from it. It was more important that my products were made with quality.

When classmates saw that I was selling Pencil Bugs, many of them wanted to help in various ways. A typical comment I heard was, "Let me help. How hard could it be to make them?" They had no idea. They were used to buying ready-made things in the store and probably never gave it much thought about the actual production of the item. I was a little uncomfortable about how to turn down their offers in the beginning but eventually I just told them it was harder than it looked to make Pencil Bugs and that I would rather do it alone. I was very particular about the way each Pencil Bug turned out.

Quality versus quantity can also be applied to donating and helping other people. After I had been donating to help foster kids, everyone seemed to be interested in how much I was giving. In the beginning, I had no idea how much to give. My dad explained that most large corporations typically only give a few percent or less which is often from their profits. I chose to donate from my gross sales.

Still, people's focus continued to be on quantity. Think about it. When the media does a story on a kid donating to any cause, the main thing they highlight is the amount donated. They are sending the message that if you cannot give a substantial amount, it does not matter. That used to bother me but then I realized that I was doing good things and it was appreciated by the people that mattered most. After awhile, I just quit telling anyone how much I was giving.

BIZ TIP: Less of a good thing is better than more of a bad thing.

A Website Doesn't Guarantee Success

When I am speaking at conferences, schools, or businesses, there is usually someone who asks about my website. They want to know who designed it, was it expensive, how long it took to get it online, and how long after I started my business before I decided I needed a website.

The first thing I tell them is that my mom designed it for me and until she got so busy helping me with Pencil Bugs, she had her own web design business. I am very lucky that my mom is available and has the creative skills to do what other people would normally have to pay for. However, even if you do not have someone that can design a website for free, there are many people that can do it for almost any budget. The most important thing is to check them out, get referrals from people who have used them, and look at other sites they have designed. When starting out, it is more important to have a simple, easy-to-navigate website that works well than a multi-page site that is unstable and too confusing to use. If you are on a tight budget, find what works for you in the beginning and you can always expand as your business grows.

One word of caution. Even if you can navigate the Internet, send emails, create documents in Word or use other software programs, do not assume that you can create a website too. It takes more than just making it look nice. Some people have made the mistake of paying for the initial design and then trying to maintain it themselves. There are so many technical aspects that unless you have the time to learn the ins-and-outs, you are better off leaving the design and maintenance to someone who knows what they are doing and has the time. Remember, if you are starting your own business, you will be swamped with a ton of other things to worry about too.

Blogs are popular and with unlimited options for design themes and layouts, sometimes it is hard to tell the difference between a site designed with traditional website software and some of the free online blog programs. Whichever you choose, make sure it is functional and the best option for your specific business.

If you are one of those people who think, "Hey, I'll just get a website up and start making tons of money," it usually does not happen that way.

BIZ TIP: A website does not mean you are going to see instant success or sales.

Whether you have a product or service business, people still need to know how and where to find you. It would be the same if you set up a physical store in the middle of nowhere. How would people find you?

You would think that it is easy to find almost anything on Internet because there is so much information available. But sometimes it works just the opposite. There is so much out there, it is like trying to find a needle in a haystack. And if you do not know what that needle looks like, it is pretty easy to miss it. Websites are the same way. It takes a lot of effort, planning, and creative marketing to get people to your site. When it all comes together, you will start seeing the results you hoped for. One thing is for sure. It will not happen overnight.

With a lot of effort, people have visited my site from around the world. Pencil Bugs products have been shipped all over the United States and Canada and as far away as China, the Philippines, Egypt, Lesotho, Denmark, and Australia. It is always fun when I get orders from another country just knowing that other people will have my products in places that I may never get to visit.

Just because your website is online, do not assume it is good forever. Weird computer glitches can happen and mess things up. Check it frequently to make sure that all of the links work and nothing has become corrupted. It is also important to update your content periodically even if you do not have new products to sell. Try to add new information or change things around a bit as often as possible. Depending on the type of business, it might require more frequent changes. Just as customers get tired of going into a store and not seeing anything new, people also get bored with websites that never change. Give them a reason to keep coming back to your website.

Remember to make your contact information easily accessible. If you want your customers to correspond via email, make sure you check it daily or multiple times a day if needed and then respond as soon as possible. Good customer service is critical to any business.

IN THE BOX OR OUT?

Very few companies can say they operate without any marketing budget at all. Pencil Bugs can. I know that things may need to change in the future but up to this point I have not spent any money on advertising. There are so many opportunities for free publicity. Take advantage of as many as possible. The key to no-cost marketing is creativity. Are you in the box or out? You cannot be creative if you follow the rules all of the time. Sometimes the craziest ideas actually work.

When you first start your business, you need to get noticed any way you can. It is important to contact all forms of media as soon as your business gets off the ground. I have used many different options. Getting publicity does not happen by accident and most of the time the media will not come looking for you. It is an ongoing process. You need to continue getting your name and business out there. Otherwise, people just might forget about you. You never want to fall off the media radar.

People usually think of media as TV, radio, and newspapers. Sometimes magazines are included too. However, there are so many more options for free publicity that people overlook.

BIZ TIP: The only bad idea is no idea.

An important part of creative marketing is brainstorming. My mom and dad are always great to bounce ideas off of. Talking with friends and business contacts can also be really helpful. If you are discussing ideas that you want to keep secret, make sure you trust the people you are talking with. You could even have them sign a non-disclosure agreement.

Newspapers: Almost every town has a local newspaper. Many also have a few free publications. I have met entrepreneurs who will not bother contacting the small-town media even if they live in that small town. They feel that it is not worth the time and effort. That is absolutely the wrong way to think. If you discount any media simply because of size, you might miss that one person who could make a huge difference for your business. There have been many times when my story ran in a local newspaper that someone in a larger market ended up reading it.

Aunt Sue subscribes to the paper and reads your story. She sends a copy to her grandkids in another state or gives them the link to the online version. One of her grandkids takes the newspaper to school to show their teacher. The teacher's friend works for a major TV station and pretty soon, you are getting a call from a producer asking to interview you.

Well, you get the point. Every type and size of media is worth the effort and even more important in the beginning.

Whenever my story has run in a newspaper or magazine, it has generated more sales and the publicity has lasted much longer than when I have been on TV or radio. Television show segments go by so quickly and most of the time you get very little airtime. If a viewer or listener is not paying close attention, your segment will be missed. They might catch your name or your business but most people will not take the time to get on Internet to look you up afterward. With printed media, people still cut out articles to save or share with someone else. Plus, everything is online now so even if someone does not subscribe to a paper, they still have access to it.

TV and Radio: Getting an interview on a major television show or news segment seems to be the golden ticket that most entrepreneurs hope for. No surprise, but those spots are not easy to get. Talk shows have specific criteria. Most of them will take segment suggestions but if your story does not fit into what they are looking for, your chances are slim. The majority of news coverage is bad news, although recently it seems that more stations are actually searching out positive stories to put on the air. Getting noticed by major news stations is still pretty difficult. You better be doing something really amazing. What you consider amazing and what the producer considers amazing may be two different things.

I have been on TV a few times with more scheduled to air in the future. One of the things that I have learned about television is that you cannot count on being a guest just because they initially contact you or show interest. Three major television shows did preliminary interviews with me over the phone. All three found me from printed media. One did follow-up interviews and asked me to send a video and my Pencil Bugs products but I was not chosen. Another decided to discontinue the segment they had originally planned. The third show was cancelled altogether before they were scheduled to tape my episode. Nothing is for sure. It is hard not to get excited if someone contacts you. However, I would advise to keep it quiet until you actually have an airdate. There are so many things that can pre-empt it. Once you have told all of your family and friends, it is so much harder to go back and explain what happened. Lesson learned.

Social Networking: Another good way to get free publicity is through social networking sites like Twitter, Facebook, or Linked In. My favorite is Twitter because it is quick and easy. It is also the one I started using first. With Twitter, even if you just take a day now and then to read what other people tweet about, you can find loads of helpful information and ideas. Then to really get the most out of it, you need to interact with people on a regular basis. That is when you will really see the value of social networking. For young entrepreneurs that are still in school, finding time to get online may be difficult. This is another example where you should probably concentrate on quality versus quantity. A little information about something worthwhile is better than too much information about nothing.

Press Releases: Press release websites are good. A lot of companies use them. Free press release sites are even better. If you can get some free advertising, why not use it? We found two free press release websites shortly after I started my business. Mom jumped on them right away. They are *www.prlog.org* and *www.i-newswire.com*. Because of a press release I posted on PRLog, I was contacted by a national TV show and many other major media sources. Normally, I will take quality over quantity. However, media coverage is one situation where the more the better. If you write a press release well, use relevant keywords throughout, and follow suggested guidelines, they really do work. At least try them. Why not? I gave you two free ones to get you started.

Press releases are good for general distribution but not for contacting specific media. It is better and more effective to send a personalized email if you are trying to pitch your story.

Blogs: Talk to ten people in business and chances are all ten have a blog. It makes sense. Blogs are just one more means of free promotion and exposure. I started my blog about the three-year mark in my business. I do not post every day. I decided when I first started that I would rather post less often and have something worthwhile to say rather than write junk every day just to be writing something.

Note: If you are a biz kid or a parent of a biz kid, make sure you choose the option that allows you to approve comments prior to posting to your blog so you don't end up with inappropriate content or links.

When I created my blog, one of the pages I made was titled, "All Posts Mom Approved." I wanted to make sure that readers knew I was not posting just anything. Plus, having another set of eyes to proofread your articles is a good idea. It looks bad if use poor grammar and make typos. Remember, a blog is a reflection of you and your business. You want to present yourself in the best way possible, not to mention that everything you put on Internet lasts forever in cyberspace somewhere. Regardless of how often you post, make it interesting so people have a reason to come back to read more.

Other people's blogs are often overlooked as another free marketing option. People are always looking for interesting stories to post on their blog.

Look for those. They are not hard to find. It is a win-win situation. The article may not get you anything immediate but you just never know who might read it at some point. Remember to reciprocate when possible. What goes around, comes around.

Magazines: When you are thinking of printed media, remember magazines. They may be more difficult to get into but many are monthly issues so your story will be around for awhile on someone's coffee table or maybe in an office lobby. Most people only think about magazines that directly pertain to their business or age bracket. If you do, you are really limiting your possibilities.

After seeing an article in the Costco Connection magazine about adult entrepreneurs, we contacted them to see if they were interested in young entrepreneurs. They loved the idea but because they had just run their article, they were not able to do a related one so soon after. We continue to keep in contact with them because you never know when the idea will fit into their schedule.

My dad travels a lot for business. On one of his Southwest Airlines flights, he happened to pick up a copy of their in-flight magazine, *Spirit*. There was an article that he thought we would be interested in. Mom and I both read it but what Mom was more interested in was who to contact about submitting my story. The magazine sat on her desk for a couple of weeks. Normally, she jumps right on those things but she was really busy so that kept getting pushed farther down her list.

A few days later, the phone rang and it was a writer for that very magazine. I think she almost fell off her chair. There has been so many times where freaky things like that have happened. It goes back to my belief that "everything happens for a reason." None of us even question how things happen anymore. We are just glad that they do.

The writer told Mom that she found me on Internet as they were searching for young entrepreneurs to interview for the magazine. I did the interview a few days later and my story appeared in the September 2009 issue.

Do not just think of the magazines you can buy at the grocery stores. There are so many other possibilities. An in-flight magazine that is in every airline seat for one month probably gets more readers than the average subscription magazine.

HARO: If you have not heard of HARO or Peter Shankman, let me introduce you. An entrepreneur himself, Peter is the founder of the free online resource HARO which stands for Help A Reporter Out. (*www.helpareporter.com*) Reporters, freelance writers, producers, and pretty much anyone else that is looking for sources can post their queries on his list. With over 100,000 subscribers to his daily list, it is one of the best sources for free publicity and media connections.

Mom subscribed to his list sometime during my second year in business. He sends out three lists per day, Monday through Friday. It is a lot of information to sift through but once you get the hang of it, it goes pretty quickly. Mom takes care of that for me while I am in school. If she sees anyone who is looking for information about entrepreneurs, she contacts them immediately. I have been featured in many articles online as well as in print due to HARO requests.

<u>Contests</u>: These can be a good source of media attention but from my experience, finding available contests for entrepreneurs is time-consuming. If you do find contests, most have a minimum age requirement which eliminates really young entrepreneurs many times. However, sometimes being creative and ignoring the rules can get your foot in the door. More on this in the chapter "Ignore the Rules."

<u>Giveaways</u>: This next idea is not actually free. Well, it is free but not for you. If you have a product business, consider giving away free stuff now and then. It does not have to be your most expensive product; just something so you can get your products out to more people. People are always excited to receive free things and are more than willing to spread the word about you and your business. That brings me to my last suggestion.

<u>Word of Mouth</u>: Talk to everyone, everywhere. Word of mouth advertising is free and is still one of the best ways to let people know who you are. You cannot be shy if you are in business.

In general, too many people are stuck in the box and only think of publicity referring to TV, radio, or printed material. If you forget about all of the other options, you just might miss out on a great opportunity.

THE IMPORTANCE OF NETWORKING

Everyone talks about networking. It seems that if you are not part of some online networking site, you are the minority. I started an account on Twitter and Facebook after I turned thirteen, which is technically the minimum age requirement for most sites.

As I was thinking about how important networking has become, I wondered what the word 'networking' meant to an older person. I decided to call my grandpa. He always has an interesting view on things.

"Hi, Grandpa. What's networking?" I did not tell him why I wanted to know.

"Well," he said. "To me, it means researching different things and getting information from a lot of other sources."

Then he talked about television networks and what it was like when they only had radio when he was young. As I listened to his stories, it was interesting to see how words have taken on new meanings over the generations.

When my parents were in college, people were encouraged to network to find jobs. The more people you knew and talked with, the better your chances were. Many people thought networking was for business only.

Then along came my generation and social networking. It is not just about making business connections anymore. Adults and kids use networking sites to keep in contact with friends and family too. In fact some people seem to forget that what they type is seen by the whole world. Do we really all need to know that their dog is chasing the cat around the house again or that the car has a flat tire? The good thing is, you always have the option to remove those people from your network if you find that they are sharing way too much personal information. I use the networking sites for my business but part of that is also getting to know people.

I was at a conference and one of the speakers asked the audience to shout out words that described their personal relationships. Lots of different adjectives were used. Then she asked people to describe their business relationships. The words were very different. She suggested that they should be more similar.

BIZ TIP: Develop friendships not just business connections.

The point was that if you develop friendships instead of just business contacts, or as I call them "bizships," you will have a much better network all around. Friends are more likely to help you out if needed whereas a business contact may think that they have to keep their distance. The speaker made a good point.

Using Twitter for my business is fun, fast, and easy. My username is @PencilBugs. My avatar is me holding a bunch of Pencil Bugs so people can recognize me quickly.

In the beginning, Mom would sit at the computer with me while I tweeted with people from all over the world. Everyone was so supportive and it seemed like they were excited to see a really young entrepreneur on Twitter.

The first time I logged on, I answered Twitter's one sentence question, "What are you doing?" In their 140-character limit, I typed, "Helping Mom look for manufacturers for my Pencil Bugs."

That is all it took. Within hours, we had a call from someone in Kentucky with information about possible manufacturers. It was almost as simple as the verse, "Ask and you shall receive," except we were not asking. People were helping voluntarily. It was a good feeling to be surrounded by people, if only virtually, that genuinely wanted to help.

I am still learning about networking and business. One of the best ways to keep up with what's new is to read other people's blogs. It takes time but there is so much helpful information available, it would be hard not to learn something new every day.

After I had been on Twitter for about six months, I decided to write a blog post offering my own networking tips. One of the ways that lets you know when people value what you have to say is how often they retweet your information. I still get excited every time someone retweets what I say. It just shows that age is not a factor in teaching or learning.

There is definitely an art to effective networking and communication. There is an abundance of online articles on how to network. Read as many as you can, especially if you are just beginning. If you think that there is not enough time to network, you are missing out. It is an important part of business and with sites like Twitter, it is easier than ever. The return on your time invested is well worth it.

ROI

When I first heard the term ROI, I just loved the way it sounded. Return on investment. What a cool concept. Most people probably use it in some financial context but I think of it relating to many different situations.

Sometimes when you least expect it, a little time invested can give you more in return than you ever imagined.

This story is the perfect example of what can come back to you for doing the simplest thing.

In early 2008, I received two emails on the same day from two separate employees working at a company called Nurture Smart in Nairobi, Kenya. They simply said how great it was to see a young entrepreneur doing such positive things. I could have left it at that and thought, 'Wow, that's cool. Someone from Kenya found my website,' but I was so curious and wanted to know how they found me.

I wrote back to both people individually and thanked them for their compliments. I told them a little more about my business in case they had not looked at every page of my website. Since I had never met anyone from Kenya, I also asked them a few questions about their company. They explained that they ran a program for kids in Nairobi to teach them basic business/finance skills and open up possibilities for entrepreneurship. I offered to send them more information if they needed.

A few more emails went back and forth and before I knew it, they had asked me to be their peer ambassador. They also invited me to be a guest speaker and judge for their annual entrepreneur competition later that year.

I could hardly believe it. Opportunities like that do not happen every day. Taking the time to respond to them made all the difference. People are important. Everyone matters.

LIFE TIP: Everyone deserves to be acknowledged and recognized.

My parents and I had many conversations with the program's founder over the next several months making plans to attend their annual event later that year. As we prepared for vaccinations, flights, hotels, and got excited about our first safari, we received sad news. Nurture Smart's partner backed out on them leaving them in a financial position where they could not continue their program.

While some people would have written them off, we did not. I knew very little about Kenya except that the kids did not have the opportunities that we do here. I liked how Nurture Smart described their program and thought that they were doing the right things by teaching the kids basic business skills. Many times, people or companies send money, clothing, or food to third world countries thinking that is the only way to help but when those supplies are gone, the people are still in the same situation they were before. They need the skills and knowledge to keep going and improve their lives. Nurture Smart is providing those skills.

We continue to stay in contact with Nurture Smart helping them find funding sources for their program. Every child deserves the opportunity that so many kids in America take for granted.

I feel very fortunate to have connected with Nurture Smart and believe that one day I will have the privilege of helping young entrepreneurs in Kenya as well as in other parts of the world.

SEE THE POSSIBILITIES

Have you ever seen a horse race or a parade where the horses wear blinders? It keeps them from getting distracted by what is going on around them. All the horse needs to do is look straight ahead at the track or street. Single focus. One goal.

Blinders are okay for horses but not for people. We can get so focused on one goal that we forget to see the possibilities around us. This can happen at any age with any situation.

One of my favorite online video games to play is Runescape. It is a multi-player fantasy adventure game that can be played very simply just for the fun of it. However, I take it to the next level where I utilize the virtual economic system of the game, set goals, find creative ways to make money and see the maximum I can achieve. I spend just as much time offline planning my strategy for certain goals as I do playing the actual game. Sometimes regardless of how much planning I have done, I still miscalculate details and miss an opportunity that was right beside me all along. It is like having blinders on. I only see what is right in front of me.

LIFE TIP: Don't limit your opportunities.

Look at another situation. Think of how many products there are because an invention went wrong. One of my favorites is the Slinky. After a spring fell off his desk, marine engineer Richard James watched it tumble across the floor until it finally came to a stop.

Had he not been open to the possibility of using it as a toy, we would not have the fun, but simple, Slinky today.

When I started on Twitter and created my own blog, I had no idea of the possibilities that would be right in front of me. I had planned on posting articles on occasion and maybe tweeting now and then. School took up a lot of my time so I thought of social networking and blogging as a side thing. The idea of writing a business book had not even entered my mind at that point. I started tweeting some business tips on Twitter and many people thought that they were pretty insightful for someone my age. That is when I realized I could write a business book from a teen entrepreneur's point of view. The possibilities were right there all along. It just took looking around to see them.

There are a million stories where someone missed an opportunity because they had blinders on. Take them off! Look around. Be open to possibilities. You might be surprised at what is right beside you.

LEARNING HAS NO AGE REQUIREMENTS OR RESTRICTIONS

To quote my grandma, "The day you stop learning is the day you die." One of the biggest mistakes a person can make is if they think they know it all. No one ever does. There is always something more to learn if you are just open to ideas and willing to listen.

Of course, saying this is much easier than doing it, especially for a kid. I will admit it. I do not always listen. As kids, we think we already know it all. That is just the way most of us are wired.

LIFE TIP: Older people can learn from someone much younger too.

Teaching and learning does not always have to be from an older person to a younger one. Take computers, for example. For many older people, technology does not come easily because they did not grow up with it. For kids, it is almost second nature. So who did most older people learn about computers from? Someone younger, of course.

Many older people, like my grandma, were thrilled to learn the computer. It gave her so many opportunities that she did not have before. It made it easier for her to become a first-time author at seventy-five when she published her book *Bikes, Trikes, Toads, and Roads: A Lifetime of Stories*. Without the computer and Internet, she probably would not have accomplished that; well, at least not as easily.

Whatever your age, if you are open to new ideas and do not have the know-it-all attitude, you might be surprised at what you can learn.

Adults never seem to say how old they are. I guess they figure it is not important. When you think about it, age is not important. You can do anything if you set your mind to it, regardless of how old or young you are.

After I had been using Twitter for several months, I wondered who the oldest person was on their site. I began tweeting asking to hear from people that were willing to reveal their age. I let them know that I was planning to write an article and also include their story in my book. Right away, I received responses from and about people in their sixties. I knew that was not very old. Although my grandma did not use Twitter or any other social networking site, if she could write a book, navigate the Internet and use email, among other computer applications at her age, I knew there had to be an older Twitter user out there somewhere.

In a very non-scientific attempt to find an answer to my question, I tweeted every day for one week asking the same question, looking for the oldest tweeter. About the fourth day, I received a response from a 76-year-old man. His name was Tom Holthaus. I was very excited. Now I was getting somewhere. I continued to tweet but was also including his username and age so people had an age baseline.

By the end of the week, no one else had responded. Mr. Holthaus was the guy. He was the oldest Twitter user I could find or at least the oldest person who was not afraid to say his age.

My casual survey obviously would not meet any scientific criteria but that was not my point. I wanted to learn from this person so I sent him a long list of interview questions. Mr. Holthaus was very willing to help me. I posted the following article on my blog on May 24, 2009.

To Tweet or Not to Tweet?

Just a few years ago, a tweet was the sound a bird made. Now with the innovation of the social networking site called Twitter, a tweet is a short note used to communicate with people all over the world. In 140 characters or less, people start friendships, share business ideas, and keep in touch with family.

As with many social networking sites, Twitter has a minimum age requirement of thirteen years old. However, there is no age limit to how old you can be. The only condition is the willingness to learn the technology.

In the five months that I have been on Twitter, I have tweeted with people of all ages. I started to wonder who the oldest Twitter user was. In a very non-scientific attempt to find an answer to my question, I tweeted every day for a week, several times a day to see what I could find. The first response I received was from a 62-year-old person. I knew that wasn't very old so I kept tweeting expecting there just had to be someone older.

Finally, a guy tweeted saying he was seventy-six. His name was Tom Holthaus. Seventy-six was pretty good but just in case there was someone older than Tom, I tweeted several more days but no one responded. Maybe there is someone older but they just didn't want to admit their age or maybe they didn't see my tweets. Either way, I wanted to interview Tom and find out more. Tom was happy to help.

On April 5, 2009, Tom Holthaus because an official tweeter because he had been hearing about Twitter on TV and it piqued his interest. He signed up using the name @tjholthaus and started tweeting from his home in Olympia, Washington.

Tom was already using MySpace to keep in touch with his granddaughter but found Twitter opened up more possibilities. Tom says he "spends eight hours a day on Twitter. He loves meeting new people and exchanging ideas."

Computers aren't new to Tom. Years ago, he worked for Xerox using computers for typical office tasks. He also worked in the aerospace industry and before retirement, he was a COO of a software company. When asked what he does in his spare time besides Twitter, Tom said he "reads books, keeps track of politics, goes target shooting, and is an active defender of Second Amendment rights."

His children and grandchildren love that he is using Twitter and constantly ask him how many followers he has. At the time of this article, Tom had 1571 followers but as any tweeter knows, that can change minute by minute.

In my interview with Tom, I asked what the most memorable event was in his life so far. He said, "My first solo flight," which is no surprise since after college, he spent four years in the Air Force as a pilot and intelligence officer.

Tom is the perfect example that you are never too old to learn something new. Twitter is one of the easier social networking sites and it has something for everyone.

Mr. Holthaus, my grandma, and many other people are living proof that learning has no age requirements or restrictions. When you think of it, getting old has its advantages. The memories that older people have must be terrific because of how much they have seen and done. They also still have the ability to learn and make new memories.

On the opposite end, there are stories about how babies can learn at very early ages. One of the common things parents teach babies is sign language or baby signs. There are many books written about this. My mom bought one of them and taught me some of the basics before I was a year old. I do not remember signing at that age but she said it made communicating with me much easier. Isn't communication what keeps us all going?

When we are little, we try everything. It never occurs to a kid that we cannot do something. It is only after we start to grow up that we think we can't or are told we can't. Even though I have used the word "can't" more than I should, I have to remind myself that I can do anything if I just take the time to learn, am open to ideas and am willing to listen. I hope I get to be as old as my grandparents or my oldest Twitter buddy, Mr. Holthaus, and that I continue to learn as much as possible from people of all ages.

LISTEN MORE THAN YOU TALK

My grandpa has a lot of stories that start out with the words, "When I was your age . . ." I guess that is a pretty common thing to say as people get older. Even at my age, I think I have said that a few times when I was talking to younger kids. When I hear myself say those words, even I think it sounds funny coming from a teenager.

One of the things that I have heard my grandpa say many times is, "When I was your age, kids were to be seen and not heard." Apparently, many people felt kids were around to get things for their parents or to change the channel on the television. Changing the channel was a big job back then. It meant that someone had to walk up to the set and physically rotate a knob. I guess now we know how they got along without remotes. They had kids.

Being seen and not heard does not sound very nice or fair. My parents have changed that a little to say, "Listen more than you talk." This applies to kids as well as adults but it is not meant to make anyone feel invisible. There is a huge benefit to talking less and listening more. I have already seen that in many situations.

I go into most new situations with caution. I like to hang back and assess things for awhile. Watch and listen before I jump in. Scope everything out first. It is amazing what you can learn by doing this.

A good time to listen more than you talk is when you have an opportunity to be around an older person. I am not talking moderately old. I mean really old, like someone over ninety. I am really lucky to have a great, great aunt who turns 100 years old this year. The cool thing is that she is not afraid to tell her age. She is healthy and can keep up with people much younger. I think she is actually proud that she is one of the few who have made it this long. She is looking forward to her 100th birthday. She will have a huge party. People will make a big deal over her. Willard Scott might announce her birthday on the Today Show. To top that, she will receive a birthday letter from the President of the United States. A person definitely deserves all of that recognition and more if they have reached a milestone like that.

Having time to just sit and listen to her stories is pretty amazing although I do not get to do it that often since we live in different states. It is hard to imagine what someone must have seen and experienced in a century of living.

I also was lucky to meet another person in his nineties - Art Linkletter. In fact, it was more than just a casual meeting. I was fortunate to have done a speaking event with him and Mark Victor Hansen, co-author of the *Chicken Soup for the Soul* series. When my mom learned that I would have this opportunity, she was so excited. Of course my first question was, "Who is Art Linkletter?"

Mom informed me that he was very famous for many years on television long before I was born. Mr. Linkletter was the originator of *Kids Say the Darndest Things* which was part of his television show.

The event with Mr. Linkletter was to promote Mark Victor Hansen's new book, *The Richest Kids in America* in which my business story was included. The plan was to have Mr. Linkletter interact on stage with some of the kids in Mark's book. As things got started, Mr. Linkletter started telling stories about his own life, how he got started in business and some of the more notable products he invented. I was so fascinated just listening to him that I did not care one bit about answering questions or getting to tell my own business story. I could have listened to him tell stories all day. It was one of the most memorable experiences in my life.

Listen more than you talk is good advice for people of all ages in a lot of situations. It does not mean that you are invisible. Listening is when you can learn the most. Questions can always come later. Try it. You will be amazed. I know I have been.

MONEY IS FUNNY

Sometimes people mistakenly assume that rich equals wealth. That is not always true. There are many things that can make you rich.

I look at my great, great aunt at one hundred years old. To people that know her, she is rich in health. From the stories she tells, she has worked hard all of her life. She and her husband lived on a farm and never had much money. Like many farm wives back then, she raised the kids by herself, took care of the housework, but also helped her husband outside with the farm chores. Two of her four children died in childhood accidents. She has pretty much outlived everyone she knows including one of her adult daughters.

Although many people could feel sorry for the life she has lived, she feels very rich. She has reached a milestone that not many people do and is still healthy enough to keep up with her younger friends. She is also very rich in a century full of knowledge.

If someone asks me how much money I make from my business or how many products I have sold or what percentage I donate to charity, I tell them that it is not about the money. Each person has an opinion about money which is relative to their own life.

BIZ TIP: Wealth is simply a perception.

If I said I were making $100,000 a year, many people would not believe it was possible from such a simple idea like Pencil Bugs. An amount like that may also deter people, especially other kids, from trying to start their own business. If something seems so unreachable, many people will not even try.

On the other hand, if I said I were only making $1,000 a year, it diminishes all of the effort and hard work I have put into my business and some people might not feel it was worth bothering.

Either way, as a young entrepreneur, I focus on how I can inspire other people to try their own ideas and encourage giving back in some way.

Money is funny. We need it to live but we do not have to share our financial information with anyone. Most of the time, it is better that we do not.

When someone asks about my business finances, I often smile and say, "Pencil Bugs is a private company but as soon as I go public, you will be the first to know." It is more important *what* I am doing rather than *how much* I am doing.

My current financial facts that I will share with you are:

- My business has been profitable since I started in 2005.
- Sales have increased every year.
- I have been donating a portion of every sale to charity since I started.
- I have never been in debt or borrowed money from anyone.
- After supplies and other expenses, the rest goes into a college fund.
- Currently, I have two employees who thankfully work for free (Mom and Dad).

BIZ TIP: If you do anything in life strictly for the money, you are doing it for the wrong reasons.

Some of you are thinking, "Money is not important to Jason because he is still a kid and does not need to support himself or anyone else."

That is true. I feel very fortunate that I have had opportunities so young and that my parents have supported my ideas. That is why I especially encourage other kids to try their ideas now because if they fail, they do not have much to lose. Making a living from their business can wait a few years. It is the perfect time to experiment with business ideas when we are young.

I have talked with a lot of adults who started their own businesses. One of the traits they have in common is the drive to become successful. They also take chances and think outside the box. Some of them started their business out of necessity and survival so making money was the main reason. Others turned a hobby into a business. A few started by accident like I did. Whatever the motivation was, they all began to pay it forward once they started making money. Give back in any way you can. You will be surprised at what you get in return.

Money is funny. My grandpa taught me three things about money.

1. Don't loan it unless you can afford to never get it back.
2. Save as much as you can – being frugal is a good thing and it's not new.
3. Don't mix friends and money.

SPEND OR SAVE?

It is not about how much money you have but how you manage it that matters more.

As far back as I can remember, I have always saved more than I spent. When someone would give me money for birthdays or Christmas, I thought about buying toys just like most kids do, but when it came right down to it, I did not want to spend it on just anything. I liked getting money, having money, but I was not so thrilled to see it go that quickly.

My parents both have the same financial values: don't spend more than you make, don't spend every dime, and save as much as you can because you never know when that rainy day might come. Be smart with money, compare prices, and look for the best deal.

One time I found a toy car in the cheap toy aisle of a drug store. It cost eight dollars which I thought was a good deal, especially since I had twelve dollars to spend. Even with sales tax, I would have some money left over. The plastic car came with a small circular, vertical, magnetic track. The car was supposed to do loops around the inside of the track without falling to the ground. I thought it would be fun and could not see any reason why it would not work as the package showed. Mom had a different thought. She saw flaws in the way that it was made and based on the price, was not expecting too much.

As most kids would do, I talked her into letting me buy it and at least I was using my own money. I was so excited to get home and give it a test run. Right before I cut open the plastic packaging, Mom asked me if I were sure I wanted it.

I continued to cut the plastic and finally freed my new toy. After making one simple snap to loop the track together, I set the car on the track and gave it a shove up one side. It fell straight down as soon as it zoomed up the curve.

Maybe I didn't push it hard enough. I tried again, this time with just a little more force. It went around the loop and the magnet held it on just fine. I played with it awhile longer but then quickly lost interest. It was pretty boring.

"Mom, this isn't as fun as I thought," I said. "Do you think the store will give me my money back?"

She looked at the cut-up plastic packaging. "I don't think so. The store would not be able to re-sell it like this."

Eight dollars down the drain and all I had was a small plastic car with a magnetic loop track. I was bugged, really bugged. I just wasted eight dollars. I should have listened to Mom.

She didn't say anything. She didn't have to. At seven years old, I guess that was one lesson she wanted me to learn the hard way. Since then, whenever I want to buy something, regardless of whose money I am spending, I wait at least two to three days and then ask myself several questions.

Do I really need it?

How much will I use it?

Is it worth the price?

Can it be returned or exchanged?

I also shop around online and at other stores to compare prices. Once I go through this waiting period,

I usually make the best decision. It is a good way to learn money management.

There have been times in my fourteen years that I wished my parents would have bought me toys or the latest gadgets that a lot of my friends had. Even when I had my own money saved up where I could have paid for something myself, my parents still said I had to get their approval first.

Did I always like that rule? No. Am I already glad they did that with me? Yes.

It pays to learn about money, spending, and saving as early as possible. Without ever receiving an allowance, I have been able to save a lot of money. It can be done. It just takes a little more effort from kids and parents.

PUBLIC SPEAKING

Public speaking is a scary thing for most people.

I started public speaking for my business at the age of ten. People have asked me many times if I were shy or scared. The truth is I was shy, scared, and a little nervous in the beginning. When I used to do a lot of Pencil Bugs sales events, I even had a hard time talking with people one-on-one. The more I talked to people and found out that most of them were very supportive and impressed with what I was doing, the easier it was to do public speaking.

I had been in business only a few months when I was asked to give my first presentation to a community organization. There were about thirty staff members in the room. That size of a group does not seem very large now because I have spoken at events with several hundred people as well as on live TV since then. But for a ten year old, thirty adults can be pretty intimidating. I was a little scared at first but when I accidentally made a joke right in the beginning, everyone smiled and laughed with me. My slip-up put everyone, including me, at ease. The rest of my talk was a breeze. I still enjoy giving presentations to anyone who invites me; community groups, libraries, businesses, schools, or large events.

BIZ TIP: Public speaking is like having a conversation in your living room but with a much larger group of people.

Unless you are giving a very formal presentation, there is no reason to psyche yourself out. Your audience is just like you. Relax as if you were talking with a group of friends. You will be amazed at how much more comfortable you are. Nervousness starts when you think too much about how you are standing on stage alone and several hundred people are all looking at you. The key is not to focus on that point.

Practice does not necessarily make perfect but repetition eases the nerves and builds confidence. For me, it is a little like acting. I get to be in the spotlight and have fun while telling people about my business. I do not memorize a speech because people can tell right away that it sounds too rehearsed. There is nothing more boring than listening to a memorized speech. You get the feeling that the person could recite it in their sleep and that they are just as bored as you are.

I still use note cards in case I forget something important but I like to adlib things now and then just to make it more fun for the audience and me.

I believe the most important thing to remember when public speaking is that the audience has come to see *you* and hear what *you* have to say. If occasionally I get nervous before a presentation, Mom gives me her pep talk. "You are the one on stage. You have something of value to share otherwise they would not have invited you to speak. You control the room."

That is all it takes to get me back on track. Mom is a good motivator although she admits that she is glad that I am the one doing the public speaking and not her.

Regardless of your age, here are a few basic tips that will help you become a better public speaker and hopefully ease the nerves a little.

1. *Know your subject and material.* It is the same advice if you are writing a book. Write what you know. The more personal knowledge you have about a subject, the easier it is to say it or write it.

2. *Practice a lot.* I admit it. I do not like this one at all. I think most kids do not even like the word 'practice.' It gives us a bad taste. It usually means less time for playing. The fact is, practice makes your presentation better. But practice does not mean memorizing. Anyone can recite something but not everyone can tell a good story.

3. *Slow down.* I cannot tell you how many times while I was practicing in the beginning that Mom reminded me to slow down when I talked. You will think you are talking at a snail's pace and sounding totally ridiculous but talking slower has many advantages. If you need a second or two to remember a point, a pause is not as easily noticed if you are already talking slower. People also tend to talk faster when they are nervous. Speaking slower gives the impression of confidence even though you might still have butterflies in your stomach. If you talk at lightning speed, you may also lose some of the audience. Like my grandma says, "Hold on. My ears can't hear that

fast." You are on stage for a reason. Give the audience time to listen.

4. *Speak up.* Chances are, if you are in a large room, you will be using a microphone. Make sure you know how to use it. If you have the opportunity to test it out before you speak, that is really helpful. Just think of how many times someone gets up to a microphone to perform or speak. As soon as the first words come out of their mouth and they hear how loud they are, many seem to have the same reaction. "Oooh, wow! That was loud!" That simple statement can make you look very inexperienced. If there is no microphone, talk loud enough so that everyone can hear you. That does not mean you have to yell either. Learn to project your voice and get someone to help with that if you do not understand how to do that.

5. *Know your audience.* I used to stand in the back of the room away from everyone as they entered and found a seat. It did not matter if it was a small group or a large room full of people. I felt uncomfortable talking with audience members one-on-one. Then one day my mom nudged me toward the door and said I should at least say 'hi' to people as they came in. Once again, she was right and her advice made me feel more comfortable. By the time I was ready to start speaking, I felt like I already knew a few people. Then during the participation portion which I usually did at schools, I had

kids that I could call on, sometimes by name, to help me. That helped them feel more involved too.

6. *Talk to the audience.* Do not stare at a spot on the wall as many people suggest. Your audience is made up of real people just like you. Look around the room and talk to people individually as if you know each person. All of a sudden you are not talking to a large audience but to a small group of people scattered around the room.

LIFE TIP: Remember, everyone makes mistakes.

While you are giving your talk, if you do make a mistake, do not worry about it or get upset. I have found that the best way to get through mistakes is to just keep going. The audience usually will not even notice. If you make a really big mistake, try to make a joke about it right then and there. You get a laugh and then you can move on.

At the end of my school presentations, I always save time for questions and sometimes I get a lot of them! It is pretty fun to hear some of the questions that come from little kids. Depending on where I am speaking and how big the crowd is, I often get kids that want to tell me all of the ideas that they have ever had. And I mean ALL of their ideas. In the beginning, it was a challenge when they went on and on. I was not sure how to acknowledge their input while at the same time, allow other kids to participate. I smiled a lot and watched for cues from Mom standing in the back of the room. No matter what their ideas were or how silly they sounded to the other kids, I encouraged them to try their ideas. It was really fun to see how excited they got at the possibilities. So many of them said they wanted to be just like me!

A single school classroom, a small business or community organization, or a large event, public speaking gets easier the more you do it.

USING NOTES

So you have to give a speech or presentation. Chances are you are nervous. No big surprise there. People might have suggested that you memorize what you are planning to say. That only puts more pressure on you. Now, not only are you afraid of getting on stage but you will need to spend time trying to memorize your speech. But that's not all. You will probably worry that you will make a mistake, if the words will come out of your mouth at all, or if you will forget what you were supposed to say. It can be pretty scary.

Since I gave my first presentation, I have always used small note cards. In the beginning, Mom would help me write my talk. (I don't use the word speech because that is too much like a school assignment or some political speech. When I give talks, it is much more casual because I want to make the audience feel comfortable.) Mom would type up notes on three-by-five index cards for me. I used as many cards as I needed. Of course, she would not write out every single word because she never wanted me to sound like I was reading a speech. Bullet points were enough to help me remember what I needed to say and make the transition to the next point. Like most kids, I am not crazy about practicing but I had to go over my notes several times so I did not end up just reading them.

As I gained more experience, I kept using note cards but I was able to use fewer cards and it was easier to just talk about what I knew while still having the main ideas written down so I would remember to cover all of them.

After Mark Victor Hansen interviewed me for his book, *The Richest Kids in America*, he invited me to speak at a few of his MEGA and book promotion events all over the country. It was always an honor and I loved being in that environment with inspirational speakers from all areas of business.

At one of his events, I met best-selling author and motivational speaker, Barbara De Angelis. I did not know who she was but when Mom said she was famous, I listened. When Barbara walked on stage, she carried a stack of papers with her. They were not even small note cards. They were half sheets of pink paper and even from several rows back, I could see that she had a lot of them.

I was surprised at how calm and casual she was. Barbara said a few words while taking a couple of steps around the stage. Then she stopped to point out her new shoes. She lifted up one foot onto the stool and then took off her shoe to show the audience the sole. The soles were so smooth that she was worried she might slip on stage. She told us how she had asked her assistant that morning to take her shoes outside and scuff up the soles on the concrete so they would have more friction. If sharing that information did not make her a regular person already, she also added that she only paid twenty-nine dollars for them.

I looked at my mom next to me and she was nodding her head and smiling. She nudged me, "See, even rich and famous people can be sensible with their money."

Her shoe story was really entertaining and made the audience have a good time and identify with her even more. Using notes probably made it easier for her to get back on topic too.

Barbara talked for a few minutes more and then surprised a lot of people. Well, at least I was surprised. She drew attention to the fact that she was using notes and made some very good points why she still uses them after all these years.

Everyone has choices with how to spend their time and money. When you go to hear someone speak, you want it to be worthwhile. You also want it to be interesting and not feel like they are reading a speech word for word.

When I am in the audience even if it is just for a classroom presentation, one of the most annoying things is when a speaker cannot remember what they were going to say. If they ramble on and on or stop altogether because they cannot remember what they were talking about, it really distracts from their topic.

As I have given more and more presentations, I have tried to use fewer and fewer notes. My original plan was to get to a point where I would not have to use any notes at all. After hearing Barbara De Angelis speak that day and seeing her use notes, I decided that using notes may be the best thing I could do for the audience.

Time is valuable and every person counts. Whenever you are giving a talk, regardless of how small or large the audience is, give them your best by being prepared, staying focused, and making it the most interesting experience you can give them.

A LITTLE NERVOUSNESS CAN BE GOOD

Whether you are giving a formal speech, a business presentation, or a musical performance, nervousness can still take over.

I gave my first solo performance on stage at the age of five. In kindergarten, my school held a talent show. Competition was tough. They did not let in just any act. Everyone had to audition in front of several teachers.

I loved singing. I always have. I guess I got my musical talent from my mom's family. Mom plays piano so she thought it would be easier for me to have her accompany me instead of trying to sing along with taped accompaniment.

She was right. After I heard some of the other kids try to keep up with their background music, I was sure glad that my mom was there for me. She could keep up with me instead of me trying to keep in time with the music.

Mom picked out the song that I sang the first year. If she had left it up to me, I would have probably picked some simple song that we learned in preschool. She already had her publicist/marketing hat on when she chose "This Land is Your Land." She thought a patriotic song would appeal to the audience. And who better to perform it than a cute little five-year-old boy?

I did not sing all the verses. The original song is very long and I found out that most people do not even know the whole thing anyway. Plus, each act had a three-minute time limit. I sang two verses and then right before I got to the chorus, I shouted, "everybody sing." The stage lights were bright and the audience was dark but I could just imagine the smiles on people's faces as I heard the *oohs* and *aahs*.

It was fantastic. A hundred people or so, all singing along with me simply because I asked them to. What an amazing feeling! Whatever nerves I might have had before or when I first walked on stage, quickly disappeared. I was so excited that everyone sang along and they clapped for what seemed like forever.

The next year in first grade, I tried out for the talent show again and was selected to perform. Once again, Mom chose the song for me. Barry Manilow has always been her favorite musician. Who knew she would have thought that one of his songs was appropriate for a six-year-old to sing? "I Am Your Child" was not the normal talent show song but my performance of it definitely made an impact on the audience, especially the parents. Mom knew what she was doing. After the performance, several moms came up to me and said that they had tears in their eyes as they listened to the words.

When we moved and I started a new school, I performed in two more talent shows. Shortly after that, I started my Pencil Bugs business. My singing turned into public speaking and giving interviews. Depending on the event, I still get a few butterflies sometimes. It is usually more because of the anticipation than the actual performance. It only takes me a sentence or two to shake the nerves. Then it just becomes fun and I know that I am on stage or in front of the audience for a reason.

Public speaking is one of the most common fears for many adults. I guess I am lucky. Starting out young has made it easier for me. Even if a person starts out later in life and needs to give a presentation, it is okay to have butterflies. You are not alone. Some celebrities say that they still get jitters now and then even after thousands of performances.

A little nervousness energy can make a better performance. If you get too comfortable, people can mistake that for lack of excitement.

You Can't Adlib What You Don't Know

Talent shows, speech competitions, or business presentations. They are all a type of performance. If you make a mistake, just keep going. Sometimes it is necessary to adlib a little. As long as you act confident in whatever you are doing, that is half the battle. Of course, it is not as easy to adlib words to a well-known song or a famous poem because many people may know it too but your reaction to a mistake is what makes the difference.

I have found that it is much easier to adlib with your own material. Even though I use note cards for my presentations, I also adlib a little. It keeps things fun and interesting for me.

The one thing I learned about adlibbing is that you have to at least know the material first. You can't adlib what you don't know. Otherwise, you are just making stuff up that might not be relevant or accurate and it starts to sound like rambling.

Occasionally, my parents and I will play our own version of an adlib game. This is good for people of any age when they are trying to prepare for a job interview, media interview, or even a big presentation, especially when there is a question and answer session involved.

Our adlib game is simple and can be done anywhere. Here is how we do it. Mom or Dad asks me random questions about my business, everything from details way back in the beginning to things that are happening now. Each time, I need to make my answer unique so it never sounds like it was rehearsed or written out. That is hard to do because I have told the same story hundreds of times.

Not many people, especially kids, like to practice. It gets old sometimes. This game gives you practical experience in a fun way and is much better than practicing or memorizing a speech or note cards.

Another game we made up was the casual conversation game. It is still practicing adlib skills but for different situations. Schools do not teach kids the art of conversation. With this game, it is a fun way to learn.

This is how it works. Someone starts talking about any topic. Remember that if you are playing with a mixed age group, try to stick with topics that are simple and that most people will have some knowledge about. As the first person who started the topic is talking, it is up to the other players to find anything they can relate to and join in the conversation. It could be something that triggers a related side thought, agreeing with the other person's point of view, or even asking a question. The object is, everyone has to participate and be an active part of the conversation, not just a listener.

I have learned so many valuable life skills since I started my business. Adlibbing when necessary and being able to carry on a conversation are two very important skills. I cannot imagine where I would be if Pencil Bugs had never been born.

Jason O'Neill

THE ART OF INTERRUPTING

"Shhh! Be quiet. Wait your turn. Don't interrupt."

There is probably not a single person that has not heard one of these statements at some point. I am sure that kids hear them a lot more than adults do.

It is good to be polite. I understand why parents teach kids these lessons. What I do not understand is why no one teaches you how to interrupt politely?

If you are in a normal conversation, most people will pause long enough to give you a chance to jump in and add your thoughts. Once in a while, you meet people who do not seem to ever need to take a breath. They can talk non-stop.

When I run across people like that, it makes me wonder a few things. Do they just like hearing themselves talk? Don't they think other people have anything to say? Could it be they are uncomfortable so constantly talking makes them feel better?

I have not analyzed any of this yet. Maybe some day I will. In the meantime, I realized that I never knew when to politely jump into a conversation. It is not something that parents teach kids. In fact, most of the time we are told not to interrupt at all.

The subject of interrupting came up one day after my parents and I were at an event. Someone was talking with us about my business. I was doing what I have always been taught to do: be polite, listen, and don't interrupt, especially when adults are talking.

Since I never knew when to interject, I was pretty much a listener throughout the whole

92

conversation with only a few occasional comments here and there or to answer a direct question.

When we got home, my parents told me that I should have spoken up more. It was not like we were talking about brain surgery or quantum physics. The topic was about my business so I had a lot to say. I just could not find the right time to jump in without feeling like I was interrupting.

Instead of my parents getting mad at me for not participating, they realized I was doing exactly what they had taught me my whole life – to not interrupt.

The most confusing part was how long to wait for someone to pause before interrupting would not be considered rude. That started a brand new discussion with my parents and an attempt to teach me some basic skills. Who would have thought we needed instructions on the art of interrupting?

It turned out that there is not a certain number of seconds for the perfect pause. No formula. No hard rules. Most of it is practice and going on instinct while still being polite.

So like the adlib and conversation games my family made up, we also play the interruption game. It is a fun way to get better at knowing what is appropriate timing.

The first time we played the game, it went like this.

Dad started talking about a topic. Mom and I held hands while we listened. When Dad would get to a point where Mom would be able to interject something without rudely interrupting, she would squeeze my hand. She let him keep talking because the point was not to really add in anything. It was only to give me a signal of when she would have been able to jump in without being rude.

Once I got the hang of that and could feel the length of pauses that seemed long enough, we went to the next step in the game.

Mom or Dad would start another topic and have a normal conversation with each other. I was supposed to find the right moment to jump in and add my two cents without rudely interrupting. It was fun and within a few minutes, it was easier to hear when the right moments were.

When people say, "don't interrupt," they are usually referring to being rude. Politely interrupting is a learned skill and even harder when you have someone that is a non-stop talker. It can be done though. It just takes practice, paying attention, and really listening.

ADMIT YOUR MISTAKES

No doubt about it. We can try and try as hard as we might but sometimes we are going to make mistakes. That is just the way it is. Mistakes are going to happen. We are all human. For me, it seems like whenever I make a mistake, if I keep thinking about it too much, I end up making more mistakes because I get so preoccupied with the first one.

LIFE TIP: If you make a mistake, get over it and move on.

Sometimes I get embarrassed depending on my mistake and who is involved. It took me a long time to finally figure out that if I can laugh at myself and even make a joke about the mistake, it helps me get over it quicker.

Many people probably think that kids make more mistakes than adults. That might be true if you are looking at how often we mess up while trying to grow up. I know I have made my share of mistakes and sometimes other people's shares too. But look at a person in their seventies or eighties or even nineties. They have lived so much longer. It seems more logical that they would have made many more mistakes in their lifetime. As with a lot of things, there is a huge difference between quality and quantity so it matters more what type of mistakes a person makes than how many.

"Learn from your mistakes." Adults, especially parents, seem to give that advice a lot. It is not hard to figure out why. Kids tend to repeat the same mistakes over and over and over again so parents use that saying to get the point across.

Sometimes I even wonder why I keep doing the same thing when my brain tells me it is not right. Thank goodness, most of the time my mistakes are not huge, life-changing ones. I seem to do stupid, little things again and again.

When I was younger, no matter how much I wanted to change the way I did something, mistakes had a way of finding me. Even if it was not a big mistake, I did not like having it pointed out to me. I guess I wanted to be perfect. Silly me!

Mom and Dad reassured me time after time that everyone makes mistakes. "It is just part of living. It's okay. You are not perfect. No one is." Somehow telling me that did not matter.

The worst part was when they said how important it was to admit your mistakes. That idea did not sit well with me at all. It was bad enough that I made the mistake in the first place. Now they wanted me to admit to it? I remember struggling with this concept. I tried everything I could think of to ignore their advice.

After at least a gazillion mistakes, repeating many of the same ones, I finally got a clue. The world was not going to end if I said I was wrong or that I messed up. Friends would still like me. People would respect me for being honest. And most of all, Mom and Dad would always love me no matter what.

I am not saying admitting your mistake is always an easy thing to do. It is just the right thing to do. It does not matter what age you are. There are a lot of people, including adults, who will not ever admit to being wrong. I have had teachers who refused to do the right thing even when students showed them proof of their mistake. That has always puzzled me because there are certain adults that you expect to be good examples. Teachers are at the top of the list, right up there with parents.

My parents are no different than anyone else. They make mistakes too. The good thing is, they try to make a big point when they do mess up to show me that even parents are human.

Note to other parents: If you want your kids to respect you more, let them see that you make mistakes and be willing to admit to them. This cannot be one of those times when you use the old line, "Do as I say, not as I do." It will not work.

LIFE TIP: The worse mistake is one that you don't learn from.

Mistakes will happen everywhere — school, home, work — and they will happen to everyone. If we never make a mistake, we are not really living. How you deal with a mistake is up to you. No one is perfect.

- Mistakes will happen to everyone, even you.
- Recognize your mistakes. If you cannot see the mistake, it will be harder to move on.
- Listen to those who are trying to help or teach you things to improve.
- Admit your mistakes. Remember you are only human.
- Work on not repeating the same mistakes.
- Don't expect changes overnight.

BELIEVE IN YOURSELF

Growing up is hard. Just ask anyone. I have heard adults say they are glad they are not a kid in today's world. Everything seems to go so fast. There are so many influences and distractions. It is hard to stick to what you believe.

Even if you are a good student, school life is difficult at times. Middle school is even more of a challenge. If kids had any social skills in elementary school, they seem to have forgotten them by middle school. Boys can be especially mean. Many of them act like they are still playing the childhood game, King of the Hill. They are constantly trying to prove who is the toughest or the best at something. Every generation has had peer pressure and each generation of kids probably thinks that their time is the hardest.

The teenage years are tough. Now take all that and add in the fact that you are a kid with a business. A young entrepreneur. That makes you different from the other kids you know. Most people just don't get it. Some even think you have nothing more than a little hobby.

It is definitely frustrating. You try to explain. People try to look interested and understand what you are doing but the blank stare tells it all. It can make you wonder if what you are doing is worth it.

What would life be like if you were just an ordinary kid? No business. No income. No extra work. No public speaking. Just a regular kid. Everyone has moments that make them wonder.

If you are lucky enough to have people in your life that believe in you, they remind you to believe in yourself. It is not easy because you are looking from the inside out. You do not always see what they see.

My parents have always believed in me. They have encouraged me with all of my ideas. They have reminded me that what others think now will not matter in the long run.

This is true for people of any age. No matter what your interests are, stick to what you believe regardless of what anyone else thinks. If you have moments or doubts, it is okay to feel bad but try not to be bugged for too long. Get going. Find your inner strength. Believe in yourself and what others think won't matter. In the end, it is all up to you.

YOU ARE ONLY YOUNG ONCE

Since I started my business at such a young age, people often ask me if I still get to be a regular kid. I have always been able to honestly answer, "Yes."

Childhood goes by too fast. At least that is what everyone says. From my perspective, it cannot go by fast enough sometimes.

"Enjoy being a kid," Mom always says. "You will have plenty of time to be an adult."

If it were up to me, I would grow up much faster but not because I am anxious to work all the time. After I began meeting people who had "made" it in business, my plan was to make enough money so that when I grew up, I could work because I wanted to, not because I had to.

I feel very lucky to pretty much have the best of both worlds right now. I have my business which has become a big part of my life and has given me opportunities I could never have imagined but I also still have a lot of time to be a regular kid.

No matter what you choose to do at any age, there will always be that chance that you could look back and wish that you had done something differently. I think most people second guess themselves at one time or another. My dad is an exception. He thinks about his decisions and is confident that he is making the right choice at the time, given all of the information he has. Then once it is decided, he does not keep rethinking it. Mom, on the other hand, not so much.

No one is perfect. We all mess up now and then. I have already made more than my share of goof-ups.

Usually mistakes can be corrected. We are supposed to learn from them. One mistake you cannot fix is if you miss out on time. Once it's gone, it's gone. Done. Over.

I have had a lot of fun in my fourteen years, not just with my business but being a kid. Sure, I want to grow up faster sometimes and skip by all of the junk that also comes with being a kid but I know I will only have this time once.

My parents strongly believe that one of the most important times in a person's life is their childhood. I know they are right even though I may not always feel that way.

Whenever I tweet on Twitter saying, "Signing off. Going to play," I get replies like "Good for you. Enjoy being a kid." or "Wish I could play more." or "You have the right idea." Just because you grow older does not mean you need to stop playing.

LIFE TIP: Having fun is not just for kids.

As I was trying to come up with a slogan for my business, I wanted to get the point across that anyone could have fun with a Pencil Bug on top of their pencil. That is when it hit me. *"Made by a kid but not just for kids"* became more than just my product slogan. Everyone should remember to make time for fun.

DON'T ASK A YES OR NO QUESTION

During the first two years of my business, I held countless direct-to-consumer sales events. Sound impressive? What that really meant was that on more weekends than I want to remember, my parents and I set up a table outside local grocery stores and had sidewalk sales.

Getting the store's permission was the easy part. They were very supportive of a kid with a business and were happy to know that I donated part of my proceeds to help other kids.

The hard part was standing at my table for two to three hours. Of course, I was not standing the whole time. We took one chair and took turns resting. My parents said that sitting gave the wrong impression to prospective customers. If I looked like I was not excited to be there, then people would not be excited to buy. They might even feel uncomfortable stopping to talk to me if I were sitting down.

Although I did not like their logic and did my share of complaining, they were right. When I started having sidewalk sales, I was only ten years old. It was not easy for me to talk with people. It was awkward making conversation. I felt nervous asking people if they wanted to buy my Pencil Bugs. Everything about it was new to me.

A lot of kids that age have probably helped sell products at sidewalk sales. Girl Scouts, Boy Scouts, school fundraisers all have kids selling something. It is definitely different when it is your own business. There is a lot more pressure and the fear of rejection is more personal.

The most important lesson that I learned from my parents while doing these sales was that I did not have to ask people if they wanted to buy. When you ask a yes or no question, it is too easy for someone to simply say "no."

LIFE TIP: A nervous smile is always better than no smile.

Instead of asking people to buy my products, I would just say "hi" with a smile on my face and a lot of excitement for my products. When I did not have to worry about hearing a "no thanks," it got easier to talk to everyone.

After saying "hi" for what seemed like a million times over and over again, Mom suggested I mix it up a little. Sometimes I would say "hello." Other times I would ask how they were doing. As time went on, my courage and self-confidence grew so I tried out more opening lines. I experimented with anything that was friendly and would get people to notice me. I learned pretty quickly that if I could get them to stop and talk, I usually made a sale. The best part was that I did not even have to say the words, "Would you like to buy one?"

When a person made a comment about how cute Pencil Bugs were or asked how I made them, all I had to do was casually ask what their favorite color was or how many they wanted. Sometimes when I was feeling very confident and a bit silly, I would notice a woman wearing a bright colored shirt. After saying a friendly "hi," I would add that I had a Pencil Bug that matched her shirt exactly and assumed that must be her favorite color. As silly as that sounded, many times it worked and she became a customer.

I was already learning about human nature by interacting in different situations and having conversations with people I just met.

Those days already seem like a lifetime ago and it has only been a few years. As hard as it was to put myself out there, the experiences will always be something that I look back on and realize how lucky I was to have had those opportunities and learned so many valuable skills early.

It is probably safe to say that there are not too many people, kids and adults included, that enjoy standing outside stores trying to sell something. However, one day when I am grown up and Pencil Bugs are as well-known as SpongeBob or any other character, I would like to get permission again to set up a table outside one of the local stores that helped get me started. But I will not sell Pencil Bugs. I will give them away to every kid that comes by.

UNEXPECTED CHALLENGES

I cannot remember how many sidewalk sales we did the first two years of my business. I do remember I did not mind it as much in the summer as I did in the winter. Even in southern California, December through February can get pretty cold, especially standing in the shade with the wind blowing.

We did as many sales as we could from March to November. The good thing was that it did not take up all of my free time.

Each year, I set a sales goal. Since I was still learning the ins-and-outs of the business world, I had a hard time thinking or even caring about goals.

As the holidays got closer, I assumed that more people would be willing to buy Pencil Bugs for gifts or stocking stuffers. When I actually thought about my goal, I figured that I would be able to reach it without any trouble. It should be easy to make up the extra sales during the holidays.

Little did I know that my plan had a major flaw. By Thanksgiving, other groups like Boy and Girl Scouts and charities of all kinds had already reserved almost every weekend through December at all of the stores that allowed outside sales.

Sometimes even when we had reserved a specific day and time, we were surprised to learn that the store forgot to write me on their calendar so we could not set up and sell as planned. On other weekends, they gave me permission only to find out that when we got to the store, they also had given other groups permission for the same day.

Having multiple people selling products or asking for donations was not the best situation for the store's customers. I was never a pushy salesman but as we all know, some people can be over the top. It was also pretty easy to see that people were only willing to spend or give so much. The competition was tough. One time a group collecting money for some charity set up their table on the other side of the entry way into the store. They were really loud and pushy which hurt my business. It was a little discouraging not selling as much that day, especially when I had an actual product to sell and they were simply asking for money. But it taught me a valuable lesson. There are all kinds of people in the world and situations that will present challenges.

BIZ TIP: Don't assume your plan will work every time.

Assuming that I would be able to sell Pencil Bugs on any weekend I chose during the holidays was a big mistake. Had I not waited until the last few months, I might have made my sales goal that year.

The next year, long before the holidays approached, I had a different plan. I contacted the stores and reserved my spot far in advance. I politely confirmed that I would be the only seller on a given day. I was determined not to be in the same position as the previous year.

I try not to take things for granted or jump to conclusions. Missing my goal that year was not life changing but it certainly was something I had to learn the hard way.

EVERYTHING HAPPENS FOR A REASON

Whether you believe in God or another higher power or have any religious beliefs at all, it is pretty hard not to think that there is a reason for everything. It does not mean that we always like what happens or that we don't ask "why" a lot of times. We may get the answer but not as fast as we would like. Most people, especially kids, just need more patience.

I have always been a "why" kind of kid. I think most kids are at some point, especially when we are really young and trying to figure out everything. As kids, we do not realize how annoying that can be to adults. I saw it from a parent's point of view one day while Mom and I were in a grocery store.

Another mom was pushing her cart up and down the aisles with a little boy sitting in the upper basket area. He was probably about three years old. She would tell him something and he would ask why for everything. I might not have noticed it at all but we passed by them several times throughout the store and each time I heard the same thing over and over and over again. "Why, Mommy? Why?"

Since I can hardly remember much from when I was that age, I asked Mom if I were like that too. She laughed and said, "Of course you were." Apparently, I have never really grown out of my "why" stage but that is a good thing. It is one of the best ways to learn. Thank goodness my parents like me being inquisitive.

However, sometimes the "why" just cannot be answered, at least not in the timeframe that we would like. That is where patience and believing comes in. I am not saying I have any more patience than the average kid but I have seen where it really can pay off to be patient.

Believing that things happen for a reason does not mean we just sit back and wait. Many times we have to make things happen but no matter how hard we try, there will still be times when something does not work out the way we planned. If you know you gave it your best shot but the results were not there, that is when you really need to believe that there is a reason for everything. Sometimes it means waiting to find out. Other times you may never see the reason.

This is a hard concept for a lot of people, especially kids. If you can find some way to not get discouraged, that is a huge start. It may take days, weeks, months or even years for the reason to become apparent.

At my age, I have not had to wait years for things to happen but I have definitely had experiences where waiting even a few hours or days has been difficult.

A simple example was one time when we were doing a sidewalk sale. Like so many times before that, it was a day that sales were low. I was ready to pack up and go home after just an hour. I kept thinking that the sale was just a waste of time. I thought of a million other things I would rather be doing. We usually tried to stay for about three hours during the busy shopping times.

One day, I had had enough. Mom gave me her usual line. "See if you can find that extra ten percent in you to stay just a little while longer." I did not want to but we stayed anyway.

As it was getting close to the three-hour mark and we were packing up to go home, a woman without any kids stopped to say "hi." I politely said "hi" back while I casually kept putting my products away. She examined my Pencil Bugs and read some of the newspaper articles I had posted on the wall behind me. I thought if she were interested in buying, she would have done it after a few minutes but she didn't.

Then to my surprise, she said she was a teacher and asked if I would be interested in speaking at her school. I had already given presentations at several schools and really liked it. I said, "Sure, just tell me when."

Mom set a date with her and she went into the store to do her shopping. In just a few seconds, the exit door opened and she was back.

"I forgot to tell you that our whole school will be buying Pencil Bugs," she said. "When you come to speak, make sure you have plenty to sell."

Some people would call situations like that just coincidences or fate, I guess. There is a reason for everything. If we keep our options open, are willing to put in that extra effort and have patience, things will turn out the way they are supposed to even though it may not be the way we planned.

That sale was just one of many situations where I realized after the fact that everything happens for a reason. If my parents would not have encouraged me to stay longer, I would have missed out on a great opportunity. Not only did I get to speak to a large audience of kids, I also made the biggest one-day sale at that time in my business.

EXPECT THE UNEXPECTED

Expect the unexpected is one of Mom's favorite sayings. Her dad used to say it to her and he probably heard it from his dad too.

When she first said it to me, it made no sense. How can you expect something if you do not know what you are supposed to be expecting? It sounded really confusing.

Mom would use that line on me when I wanted to put off work.

"I'll have time to do it later," was my usual response.

"Expect the unexpected. You don't know what might pop up," Mom would repeat.

I have always been a good student, making top honors since third grade. For the most part, I do not mind doing homework and I actually like school. Most people procrastinate because they do not like what they have to do. That was not a problem for me, at least not with school.

In fourth grade after I started my business, things began to change. The unexpected happened more often. I finally realized what Mom meant.

For the first several months, I was only making small quantities of products at a time. I put up my website as soon as I started my business but since I was unsure how sales would go, I only made products as I got orders. It seemed like a pretty reasonable plan and it worked fine most of the time. It did not interfere with school work or time for playing.

As I received more media attention, orders were coming in faster than expected. My "as-needed" plan was not working so well anymore. I would have my homework schedule for the week and any extra things we needed to do and everything was fine. Then all of a sudden, multiple orders would come in putting a wrench in my system.

I loved the fact that business was good and getting better and more people were ordering my products. Managing everything and not being surprised at the last minute became a challenge though. Mom was happy to remind me, "Expect the unexpected."

The first change we made was to set up a production schedule to make hundreds of Pencil Bugs at a time, mostly on weekends. We also improved our assembly line which consisted of Mom, Dad, and me. We found ways to do things more efficiently. Those changes helped a lot and I finally realized what Mom had been talking about for so long.

Unexpected situations will always come up no matter what you are doing or how organized you are. It is how you prepare for the unexpected situations and handle them once they happen that makes the difference. Will you be ready for whatever happens at the last minute or will you freak out not knowing what to do? If you give yourself extra time, things run much smoother in the long run.

LIFE TIP: The easiest way to be ready for anything is not to procrastinate.

In 2008, we visited my grandparents in North Dakota for Christmas. That is when I realized why my mom and her family always used the saying, "Expect the unexpected." North Dakota winters are usually freezing cold, snowy and icy. If you want to go anywhere, you have to be prepared. You have to allow extra time in case the roads are bad. You take a blanket or two in the car just in case you get stranded somewhere. You watch the weather channel every day like clockwork. Nature is unpredictable so you have to be prepared for anything. When you live all your life in a climate like that, I guess you get used to the unexpected.

"Save it for a rainy day," my grandpa would say. "You never know what you might need that money for."

Lots of people, including kids, spend whatever money they earn. The more they have, the more they spend. Then when the unexpected happens and they need extra money, they do not have it.

School, work, weather, finances. You name it. There are so many examples and areas of life where you could apply this philosophy. There are no guarantees and you cannot control everything but at least you have a better chance if you are prepared.

THE POWER OF WORDS

My mom had an old copy of this poem stashed away somewhere. The author was unknown and there was no title but I thought it said a lot. I liked it so much that I had to include it in my book.

> DID is a word of achievement.
> WON'T is a word of retreat.
> MIGHT is a word of bereavement.
> CAN'T is a word of defeat.
> OUGHT is a word of duty.
> TRY is a word for each hour.
> WILL is a word of beauty.
> CAN is a word of power.

Think of the excitement a five year old has when he yells, "I DID it!" after tying his shoe all by himself for the first time. Picture the look on his face as he runs from the bathroom shouting, "I WON'T take a bath!" I remember saying things like these. They are very direct.

Each word in the poem is just as meaningful and important as the next. For me, the hardest one to say and believe is the last one — CAN.

I once heard someone say, "I am an American. I can." Interestingly enough, the last four letters in American are I CAN. That got me to thinking. Regardless of what someone's views are about politics, government, or religion, being an American with all of the privileges and opportunities we have, we should all be saying "I CAN."

There were many times when I wanted to give up on my business. I used the word "can't" a lot. Being a young entrepreneur has not always been easy or fun. I am thankful that I have always had my parents there to support and encourage me.

Once I changed the "can't" to "can," the business became much easier. I looked at things differently. I listened more and argued less. I could finally see all of the opportunities that were ahead of me once I had a different attitude. The easier it became, the more fun I had. The more fun I had, the easier it was.

I do not know everything. The one thing I do know is that when you have the "I can" attitude, you are more motivated and can do anything you set your mind to.

After reading the poem, I wrote my own.

SUCCEED

If I think I can, I'll try.
If I think I can, I will.
If I think I will, I did!

DON'T PROCRASTINATE

I am the first to admit that I sometimes put things off longer than I should. I am a kid. That's what we do.

Apparently adults are not that much different. I bet there are many people that would choose play before work if they could get away with it. Of course, there are the exceptions. My grandpa is one of those people. He still would rather go outside and do some work around the ranch than sit and do nothing.

"Don't put off doing your work if you have time today," Grandpa says. "You just never know what might happen tomorrow if you wait."

Grandma then adds her two cents. "Tomorrow is not a promise. Make the most of today."

My mom never seems to procrastinate. She hates waiting until the last minute for anything. Dad teases saying her idea of late is being on time and her idea of on time is being at least ten minutes early. His teasing does not bother her because she is proud of the way she is. "It builds credibility," she says. People know that when you say you will be there at a certain time or get a project done by a deadline, they can count on you.

She lives by her POPE method. She is not Catholic and it does not have anything to do with religion at all. It stands for Prioritize, Organize, Plan, and Execute. The result gets things done.

I hate to admit it too much but she is right. There have been times with my business that I did not want to prepare for a presentation or spend the weekend assembling Pencil Bugs.

"The presentation is two weeks away and we have plenty of products in inventory," was my usual argument.

Sure enough. Something would happen that was unexpected making it very difficult to get things done on time. I guess for most of us, it takes more than a few close calls to make us change our habits.

All I know is that waiting until tomorrow usually does not work.

What to Do?

Did you ever have a to-do list with only one thing on it? Easy, right? So you take your time and leave it until later. I have been in that situation many times even though my mom has done her best to teach me that it is not a good habit to have.

Putting off just one task does not mean you are lazy. It does not necessarily mean you are a procrastinator either. It is simply your mind playing tricks on you. Your eyes only see one item on the list. One simple thing. No big deal. You tell yourself it will not take that long so you can wait until later. You do something else instead.

I have done that a million times. I could always think of a hundred other things to do besides that one chore or assignment on my list. Have you ever noticed that a to-do list never has fun things on it? We do not need to write those down. Who would ever forget about something fun? Like most people, I only write down things that I am not that excited about doing. Otherwise, I would forget them for sure.

Getting that one thing done is harder than it seems. Pretty soon, the day is over and that one task is still on the list. Where did the time go? What did you do all day? It doesn't matter. Your to-do list looks the same.

Now, take a day when the to-do list is a mile long. Some days my list is filled with homework, interviews, and business work. When I look at it, my first thought is, 'How am I ever going to get it all done?'

The first step is to break it all down. Instead of looking at a list with ten things as one whole list, think of it as ten small parts that all need to be done. Tackle them one at a time.

I am always trying to improve how I organize and prioritize things in order to get them done. For quite awhile, I thought I had a good system worked out. I wrote everything on a white board. No matter how many things were on my list, I would start on the hardest job first. It was overwhelming if I knew that I had saved the worst for last. As I would finish each task, I would erase it. Simple. Done. I did not even have to look at it anymore. The funny thing was, I never felt like I made much progress. Even though the list was getting shorter, it still looked like a new list every time. I realized that my system needed tweaking.

Here is a trick I learned from my mom for tackling a to-do list no matter how short or long it is. Once I got over being stubborn and was willing to try something new, I found that her system worked really well.

As you write things on your to-do list, prioritize them. Of course, you will need to do the ones that have an immediate deadline first. So far, so good. I did that with my system too. The next step is where the difference came in. Do not erase an item as you finish it. Make a checkmark beside it or line through it but make sure you leave it on the list. After you complete the immediate ones, instead of tackling the biggest job next as I used to do, whip through as many of the smaller, easier ones as quickly as you can. Now with more checkmarks or lined-through items, look at the list and see how much you have accomplished. It is a much better feeling.

When I used my erase method, it was too easy to forget what was on the list in the first place. Even though the list may have gone from ten things down to six, every time I looked at it, I still saw a whole list. It was just a mental trick my mind was playing on me but it made me think I was not making any progress.

Once you try this, you will probably find that you can actually get more done even if you have a dozen things on your list. If you are organized, can prioritize and not procrastinate, it is amazing how many things a person can accomplish.

When you have a lot of responsibilities, the best thing to do is to just get started. The to-do list will not get any shorter by starring at it or ignoring it. The more you have on your list, the more you can get done if you set your mind to it.

The next time you have just one thing on your to-do list, do not get too excited thinking you have all day to get it done. At the end of the day, you might be disappointed at the outcome.

On the flip side, do not be discouraged if your to-do list is a mile long. You may find that you are more organized and can accomplish much more than you give yourself credit for.

It worked for me. When I have a long list, instead of thinking I will never get it all done, I tell myself that it is just a bunch of small things. I jump on the first one as soon as I can and tackle the rest one at a time.

No Guarantees

I have several more years until college. I do not have to worry about looking for a job right now or supporting myself. That is probably the best part about being a young entrepreneur. We can gain the business experience but also can take it slowly and hopefully not make too many mistakes. Even if we do, chances are they will not be critical.

What about the people just graduating from college now? After spending several years to get a basic degree, there are still no guarantees. Then if someone wants to get into a specialty, it means even more years of college. Now calculate how much all of that will cost. If time and money is not a big enough factor to consider, will there be jobs available?

People have already started asking me what I plan on doing when I grow up, where I will go to college, and what degree I will get. At fourteen, I am not sure about college. It does not guarantee a job or security. It is not the golden ticket anymore. It is like playing The Game of Life. If you choose the college path, all you are guaranteed is that you will have loans to pay back. It does not mean you will get the best job or make the most money. I know I could learn a lot from going to college but look at how many people cannot find jobs or have lost jobs even with college degrees. Being an entrepreneur and starting your own business is not for everyone either. There are a lot of risks involved and also no guarantees.

LIFE TIP: Be practical and use common sense above anything else. Not everything is written in a textbook.

I have experienced situations in elementary and middle school when I wondered if all of the effort I put into a project or other assignments was worth it. There have been many times when I went above and beyond the assignment. The teacher and the other students agreed that my project was the best. At first I felt pretty good about doing the best job in the whole class. I knew all of my hard work and effort would pay off.

As expected, I always got an A on the projects but so did many other kids that clearly, and admittedly, spent a fraction of the time and turned in a halfway project. But still, they also got an A.

Does that make any sense? The person who did the best work should get the highest grade, right? Whoever is the most qualified gets the promotion or the job, right? Does a college degree really make a difference, especially today? Apparently, not true. So what do you do?

Some people might quit trying so hard. Others might just keeping doing what they have always done and take whatever the outcome is.

Grandpa has no shortage of sayings for various situations. "You have to be smarter than the average bear," he says. Then Grandma adds, "Learn as much as you can. The more well-rounded you are, the more options you will have." What a lot of people forget is that learning does not have to take place in school. Sometimes the best education happens from real life experiences.

As a teenager living in a difficult economy, I can see my generation will have to be more creative, be open to possibilities, and be willing to make our own opportunities.

Some entrepreneurs say that these bad economic times are actually good for business. It forces companies to get more creative in order to stay in business and make it better. The ones that keep doing the same old things as they have always done in the past will have a harder time.

Regardless of your age, the only thing you can control is you. You are your own guarantee.

CREATE YOUR OWN JOB

What does a fourteen year old know about working for a company? Not much. In many states, we cannot legally work for someone else until we are sixteen. Then the options are somewhat limiting. We are still in school, have homework to do, maybe some extracurricular activities, and of course, friends and a social life.

Getting a part-time job is about the best we could hope for in order to still have a normal childhood. Fast food cooks or order takers seem to be a starting point for many kids. Waiters, dishwashers, bus boys, or hostesses at sit-down restaurants are a step up for some. An occasional opportunity at a department store may be an option but you do not see many high-school kids in those jobs. Working for an hourly salary does not have to be your only option. This applies to adults too.

BIZ TIP: Sometimes the perfect job doesn't exist until you create it yourself.

"Just because a position doesn't exist, doesn't mean you don't go after it," Mom says. She did exactly that with one company she worked for.

It was during the early nineties before I was born. The cell phone industry was really buzzing. Mom was working as an executive secretary in a different industry and was not too happy with her job. So like a lot of people, she watched the newspaper for job postings while she continued to work. Mom changed companies several times in her career but she never left one company until she found the next one.

BIZ TIP: Be financially smart. Don't quit your current job until you find a new one.

    A well-known cell phone company kept running big ads every week in the paper looking for engineers of all types and other technical people. After a few weeks of seeing the same ads, the light bulb went off. Why weren't they looking for support people? If they were hiring the technical people as fast as it seemed, Mom thought they would eventually need more support staff too.

    She did not waste time waiting for the company to post ads once they finally figured out they needed to hire extra support people. She sent a letter and her resume to the vice president–bypassed the normal Human Resources chain of command–and explained what she realized by watching their newspaper ads. After making her point, she suggested they interview her.

    She received a call within a day or two from the vice president personally. Mom was confident that she would be hired but never expected that he would offer her a position as his assistant before the interview was even finished. He already had an assistant and was not looking for someone new but her creativity impressed him. He admitted that he had never had anyone apply for a job that did not exist. Within two weeks, she was enjoying her new job and was especially proud of how she got it. I have heard this story many times because

Mom likes to encourage people of all ages to think past what they see.

Dad had a similar situation. He was seventeen, still in high school and wanted to earn some money. He and his friend walked into a sporting goods/clothing store and Dad asked to talk with the owner. In those days, many owners actually worked in their stores. The man said that he did not have any openings for sales clerks or anything else for that matter. Dad convinced the owner to let him work two hours for free. At the end of that time, Dad was sure the owner would find a position for him. If not, the owner would have had some free help for a couple of hours.

Dad's friend left telling him that he would never get a job that way. As Dad hustled around the store, stocking shelves, cleaning up, sweeping the sidewalk, and even making a sale, he noticed the owner talking with the manager several times. When the two hours were up, the owner agreed that he would make a position for my dad.

Within a year, they promoted him to store manager. He worked there two more years while he attended a community college and finally resigned when he transferred to another city to finish his four-year degree.

Job possibilities are everywhere. You need to be creative to find them sometimes.

If you are a kid, you do not have to wait until you are older to start earning money. And you do not have to work for anyone else. You can create your own opportunity by becoming an entrepreneur. Starting a business does not have to be really involved, especially in the beginning. In fact, it is better to start out slowly and learn as much as you can along the way from the ground up. When you are thinking about what type of business to start, remember to keep your options open and look at all of the possibilities. Sometimes the best opportunities are the ones you least expect.

Being an entrepreneur will not always be as easy as clocking in and out at an hourly job but it will definitely be more fun. The only limitations you will have are the ones that you put on yourself.

If starting a business is not for you, remember you can still create your own job with a company even if they have not thought of it yet. Think about your talents and skills and convince the company they need you. You do not have to wait for them to advertise a job. The best opportunity may not even exist until you create it.

STICK TO YOUR BELIEFS

Right before the end of seventh grade, one of our English assignments was to write a persuasive essay. The subject was, "Should the school day be one hour longer?"

I assumed that if the school day was longer, that would shorten the total number of days in the school year so that we would not have school into the middle of June as we do now. I was all for adding an extra hour to the day if it meant ending school in May and I had my arguments ready for my choice. Then the teacher explained that longer days would not mean that the school year would end sooner. It just meant more school hours each day. Once I heard that, my position changed immediately.

Having all of the information for the assignment, it was pretty easy to write my argument. As I was making notes and thinking about what I wanted to say, I decided to tweet on Twitter about it. I wondered what other people's views were. It was not going to change my opinion. I was just curious.

I only received a few responses but one bothered me a little. The person suggested that I should agree with lengthening the school day because taking that side would make me stand out from the other kids and give me an automatic A+, assuming that teachers would want longer days also.

I thought about it for awhile and then tweeted back. It was not about getting an automatic A. I knew no matter what side I chose, I would be able to write an essay that deserved an A. Taking sides with the teacher, assuming she wanted longer days, was not the answer either. Telling someone what you think they want to hear will not get you very far in life. It may be a temporary fix but in the long run, the truth will eventually come out.

LIFE TIP: Stand up for what you believe in even if you are the only one standing.

Sticking to your beliefs is not always the easy thing to do. A lot of times you will be the odd one out even if you are doing the right thing. I have had my share of situations in school when it was really hard to step away from the crowd. The consequences are not always fun and sometimes it can be pretty lonely.

Standing up for what you believe in will be challenging throughout your whole life. The sooner you get used to doing it though, the easier it becomes.

SURPRISE YOURSELF

When you think of a surprise, it is usually for someone else. How could you surprise yourself anyway? You would already know about it. It wouldn't be much of a surprise. That is not the kind of surprise I am referring to though. Give yourself the opportunity to be surprised at what you can accomplish.

When I was thinking about designing Pencil Bugs greeting cards, I was not exactly sure what they should look like. I wanted to hire an illustrator but that did not work out. My mom had some initial ideas and encouraged me to sketch one. Even though I do not consider myself a very good artist, I was really surprised with my first sketch. It was pretty good.

Then mom scanned my drawing, colored it on the computer, and before long, my first Pencil Bugs greeting card was complete. Two more designs quickly followed with Mom's help. Andy Apple, Betty Blue, and Gus Grape sat boldly on the front cover of three different birthday cards, each with a clever verse inside.

I remember thinking it would have been easier to hire a professional to design them but once they were done, I was glad we did it ourselves. I certainly surprised myself. The feeling of accomplishment and pride gave me the confidence I needed to continue creating more cards for other occasions. Before long, each of the eight Pencil Bugs characters had its own unique card, perfect for someone special. I also created a special Santa Bug Christmas card which was a big hit.

Once I had my own greeting cards, I posted a survey on my website to see what people's shopping habits were when it came to greeting cards. I probably should have done the survey before I designed the cards but I wanted to add them to my other products anyway. I was convinced I would sell them somewhere so I was not too worried.

Since e-cards were so easy and readily available on any number of websites, not to mention that many of them were free, I wondered how many people still bought printed cards. The survey results showed that enough people bought printed cards whether it was in a retail store or through a send-out option online. Either way was fine with me. I got right to work and added them to my product page with plans to eventually get them into stores.

A few weeks later, I was speaking at a large event and was able to set up a product table. It was the perfect opportunity to give the little guys a test. The sales results were a nice surprise. I had sold more than expected. I decided that I was not such a bad artist after all and the greeting cards were a good product to add to my Pencil Bugs line.

Because I saw success with my latest addition, I went ahead and created two more products — Pencil Bugs party invitations and thank you cards. They were much easier and faster to design because I used existing graphics of the Pencil Bugs. It was fun scattering Bugs all over the card while still leaving room for the necessary text.

One of my future plans is to have Pencil Bugs licensed party packs which will include invitations, cards, paper plates, napkins, cups, and decorations of all kinds — everything for the perfect party.

Try your ideas. If you give yourself as many opportunities as you can to try new things, you might like the results. So go ahead. Take a chance and surprise yourself.

YOU ARE NOT YOUR BUSINESS

How much do you really remember from before you were nine years old? It has only been five years for me and I do not remember much except for special events. I went to school, did homework, took Tae Kwon Do for several years, tried out a few team sports for a couple of seasons, and played with friends. I was a normal kid just like everyone else I knew.

When I formed my business right after my tenth birthday, a whole different phase of my life began. Pencil Bugs became a big part of my life even though I still went to a regular school, did homework, and played a lot. As far as I was concerned, I was still the same. Just Jason.

Shortly after my first newspaper interview, people were referring to me as "the Pencil Bugs kid." Sometimes they would remember my name too but Pencil Bugs was probably more memorable.

Now that I am older and have learned a lot about business, I realize it was probably a good thing that people called me "the Pencil Bugs kid." I did not know it then but I was actually building a brand name and it was quickly becoming recognizable.

About two years after I had been making and selling Pencil Bugs, I was getting a little tired of doing the business even though I had a lot of great opportunities and was having fun. I thought about quitting on many occasions.

BIZ TIP: Keep going even if you want to quit sometimes.

My parents and I talked a lot about the options. They admitted that they were tired sometimes also. It was hard and very time-consuming to make my products and keep everything going. While I was in school every day, Mom kept very busy with all of the day-to-day Pencil Bugs business while Dad worked at his own job.

After a lot of discussions, we agreed that we would not close up shop right away because we still had a large inventory of products. Instead, we would just wind it down as we sold out of the remaining products. Mom was not going to look for new marketing opportunities or media coverage either. I was still torn about the decision but I was willing to let it just fade away. That was in December of 2007.

In January, 2008 when my mom received an email from a reporter at Forbes, I took it as a sign that I should keep going. They were creating their first Top 10 List of Role Models 18 and Under. They wanted to include me!

I had never heard of Forbes before that. I had no idea how important it was. Once my dad explained it to me, all I could say was "WOW!" To be on a Forbes Top 10 list was really an honor. I was only twelve years old. How many kids could say they were in Forbes? Never in my wildest dreams would I have expected to be in Forbes for anything. Then to be viewed as a role model for kids all over the world was amazing.

Their list of "young people to admire" included celebrities, athletes, and other awesome kids. When the article came out on their website, I was amazed at who was on the list. Celebrities like Miley Cyrus, Nick

Jonas, and actress Abigail Breslin to name just a few. Olympic gymnast, Shawn Johnson, was also included before she won a gold medal in the 2008 Olympics.

Our plan to close my business only lasted a couple of weeks. It is funny how things happen when you least expect it. After being on a Forbes list, there was no way I could give up my business. Once again, I was "the Pencil Bugs kid."

2008 started out with a bang. The rest of the year continued to be very successful although I went back and forth on my decision several times. Even though everything may be going well, I think people still get tired of what they are doing sometimes. It does not matter if it is school, a job, your own business, or even playing your favorite game, it can still get old. Kids probably experience this more often since we do not always have the most patience.

Over the summer, I talked with my parents a few more times about letting the business die down. The discussions were a little different. They did not always like parts of the business either but they could see the bigger picture and more opportunities were coming my way. We had started working with different manufacturers trying to find the right one to mass produce Pencil Bugs. I wanted to expand into retail stores and I could not do that if we were still hand making them.

My parents could see the possibilities if we just kept working at it. They reminded me what I said I wanted–to make a Pencil Bugs empire, as big and as popular as any other character product on the market with toys, books, games, cartoons, and even *Pencil Bugs: The Movie*. All of my big plans did not seem to matter to me at those moments. I was tired of being "the Pencil Bugs kid."

LIFE TIP: Remember the big picture when you get tired of the small day-to-day things.

Dad suggested I write down a pros and cons list. If I saw it on paper, maybe it would help me decide once and for all. It didn't. The reasons to keep the business going were always much better than the reasons to quit but that did not change my gut feeling. Since my parents never forced or pushed me to do my business, they said it was up to me and if I really wanted to quit, they would support my decision.

Even though most kids think they know more than their parents and want to make their own decisions, we really do want help when it comes right down to it. It was really hard to decide.

"What will I do if I don't have Pencil Bugs?" I asked them. "That's who I am."

Right away, they both said, "Pencil Bugs is *not* who you are. It just happens to be part of what you have done for the last three years. It does not define you. If you stop your business, you will still be Jason. You will go on to do other things in your life and you can do anything you set your mind to."

The light bulb went off. It finally made sense. I was just a regular kid that got very lucky in starting a business at an early age. I had many fun opportunities and attention that most kids and many adults never have. But I was not Pencil Bugs. I was me.

Once the idea set in that I am *not* my business, the pressure was off. I enjoyed having my business and the opportunities. I wanted to continue working at expanding it in hopes that someday I would reach my goal of a Pencil Bugs empire. However, if that did not happen or I decided to move on from it, I would still be Jason with many other opportunities ahead of me. After all, I was still a kid.

If you believe that you are your business, you are limiting your opportunities. You have so much more to offer if you are willing to look around and be open to ideas.

PRIDE DOESN'T ALWAYS COME NATURALLY

"You should be so proud of yourself." You hear it but what if you don't feel it? You might have done a really great thing but for whatever reason, you just do not get that feeling of pride.

I recognize that I have done some pretty amazing things in my life. I have always been an honor roll student and have won many awards in school. Since I started my business, I have been donating part of my money to help other kids. People tell me that I am a good role model and being named to the *Forbes* Top 10 List of Role Models reinforced that. With all of those accomplishments, how could a person not feel proud? Sometimes I ask myself that too.

My parents are very encouraging and extremely proud of everything I have been able to accomplish. They are always telling me that I should feel proud of what I do but simply telling someone to feel a certain way cannot make it so. You can lead a horse to water but you can't make him drink. It is the same with people and pride. The feeling has to come from inside.

I wondered what the magic is that makes a person feel proud. The answer came to me one night over the weirdest situation.

While many kids younger than me stay home alone or babysit other kids by themselves, my parents did not feel comfortable leaving me home alone until a year or so ago. I did not really like the idea of staying home alone either. I guess it is different if you have siblings but being an only child and totally alone in the house, even for an hour or so, was a little creepy at first.

One night, my parents needed to go to a meeting at school. They would not be gone long and I had some homework to do anyway. Right after dinner, they reminded me to get my homework done first. They were running late so they left the dinner dishes all over the counter.

I finished my homework pretty quickly. Mom said that when I was done, I could play on my Playstation for a little bit. I looked at the mess by the sink and decided to wash the dishes instead of playing right away. It was almost eight o'clock. I knew that if I spent time doing the dishes, I probably would not have time to play at all before they got home. For whatever reason, I decided to help out anyway.

To some kids, washing dishes is probably one of their normal chores that they have to do all of the time. Not me. I have other chores that I do. Once in awhile Mom will ask me to help dry silverware or something but I had never washed dishes on my own.

Right after I had put everything away in the right places, Dad called to say the meeting started thirty minutes late. It was going to be another forty-five minutes or so until they would be home. Even though I was starting to miss them, I was kind of glad that I had more time. I had finished my homework, washed the dishes and put them away, and now still had time to play and talk to my friend on the phone.

When Mom and Dad got home, they were both really surprised at what I had done. Right after a big thank you and a hug from both of them, they told me how proud they were of me. I guess I was grinning from ear to ear because Mom said that she could see I was proud of myself too.

The next day it hit me. I had done a lot of good things before, had been an inspiration for many other people, and achieved more in my fourteen years than some people do in a lifetime. I had some pretty big accomplishments but throughout my whole life, I have always had my parents encouraging me, nudging me, and sometimes even pushing me to keep going when I wanted to give up. Let's face it. Kids do not always want to put in a lot of effort sometimes.

The night when I was home alone was the turning point. Getting my homework done, washing the dishes, and cleaning up the kitchen instead of playing was my decision. My effort alone is what got the job done. I felt really proud!

Pride comes from inside. Nobody can make you feel it. You cannot even teach someone how to feel it. When you get the feeling of pride all on your own, it is overwhelming.

EVERYTHING IN MODERATION

Moderation can be applied to almost anything: working, eating, exercising, or even playing.

Some people think that if a little is good, more is better. That is not always true. I can think of so many examples where a little bit is actually better than a whole lot. Sometimes we do not realize that until after the fact so we have to learn that lesson the hard way.

LIFE TIP: Keep it in perspective. Don't overdo it.

"Everything in moderation," Grandpa says. In his eighty-six years, he has seen what happens when people overdo something, even if it is their favorite thing in the world.

One of my biggest challenges with moderation is playing video games. Although I do not have all of the latest game systems or games, some of the ones I do play can be pretty all-consuming. My parents set limits on how long I can play on the computer because they know it can be hard to monitor myself sometimes when I get into the game. If playing for thirty minutes at a time is fun, then playing for three hours would be even more fun, right? Most kids will not ever admit that they can overload on a video game. Many of my friends do not even have limits on how long they can play. All I know is that when my parents allowed me to play as long as I wanted one day, it definitely had a negative effect on me. No matter how fun something is, too much of a good thing can become a bad thing.

Everyone could find something that they have overdone at least once in their life. Think how much better it would have been if you had just done it in moderation. Something to think about as my grandpa says.

Grandpa has lived his whole life with a little bit of everything and not too much of anything. He must be doing something right because he can count the number of times on one hand that he has needed a medical doctor. He does not believe in vitamins because he eats a little of everything including many of the foods that supposedly are not healthy for you.

I like Grandpa's philosophy. A little bit of this and a little bit of that is what keeps life interesting. A piece of bacon will not hurt you but you would not want to shovel down a few pounds of it. You have to use common sense and the brain that God gave you.

People can control how much they do but Mother Nature doesn't understand moderation. Think of the rain storms that certain areas get where whole towns get flooded out. People want the rain but not so much that it causes destruction. Even if you live in a warm climate, if you watch the weather channel for a few days in the middle of winter, you will see the effects that too much snow has on people and animals.

Visiting my grandparents' farm in North Dakota during Christmas vacation was fun but in 2008, I saw why Grandpa believes so much in moderation. While we were there, they had enough snow to dig out a large snow fort in the side of a ten-foot snow bank. That was the first time I had ever seen that much snow in one place. If they had twenty feet of snow, it would have been fine with me. The more, the better. Naturally, I thought it was awesome but all I was doing was playing in it. I did not have to trudge through the deep snow in order to feed the cows or check to make sure the water tanks had not frozen over.

"A little snow is fine because when that melts, we get the moisture we need in the spring," Grandpa told me. "But if we get too much, it causes all kinds of problems."

The day after we flew home, they had another snow storm. And then another and another. Within a few days, they had several more feet of snow. The snow fort that we worked so hard to dig out and build was starting to disappear. In the days that followed, more snow dumped until the opening to the fort was not visible at all. That could have easily been fixed by removing the extra snow but there was a bigger problem. The weight of the new snow on top of the snow bank finally caused the whole fort to collapse. The amount of the first snow was just fine. It was the excess that caused the destruction.

We cannot control nature or even other people. We can only control our own actions. Whether you are an entrepreneur working long hours to get your business off the ground, a student studying for hours on end, or a mom who forgets to take time for herself once in awhile, remember my grandpa's motto, "Everything in moderation."

NOT LIKE ANYONE ELSE

I am never going to be like anyone else. I can admire other people and aspire to do great things as they have but I will always still be me. Just Jason.

Being an only child has its advantages. Other kids talk about how their parents compare them to a sibling. It must be hard especially if you are the one that is always trying to be as good as your brother or sister.

Parents say they do not mean to compare and put pressure on one child to be like another but it happens. To be fair, it is not just grown-ups that compare people. Kids do it too. Everyone does it at some point. It is not necessarily a bad thing either. A little competition can be a good thing. It can be what keeps us going when we want to quit. How many times have you thought, "If he can do it, so can I?"

We all need a little push or extra motivation once in awhile. Just remember to be who you are. Unfortunately, some people do not know who they are, what they are good at, or what they want to be when they grow up. I have asked myself those questions already.

My parents remind me that I have a long time to figure out what I want to do but I do not have to figure out who I want to be. I am already me. I will always be me. Once you get that part figured out, you can do anything you want to do.

LIFE TIP: Like yourself for who you are.

When I went from elementary school to a new middle school, I was excited because it was my chance to leave the old Jason behind. By the time I was ready for sixth grade, I realized that I had done a lot of silly things in elementary school. Kids thought of me a certain way. To fit in, I tried making jokes and kidding around. Most of the time, it backfired and the joke was on me.

Starting middle school and being older and smarter, I was not going to make those same mistakes in a new school with new kids. Unfortunately, before long until I found myself in the same situation, trying to fit in but not doing such a good job.

I guess I was afraid that if I were just me, kids would not like me as much. My attempt at joking and kidding around did not work. Kids just didn't get me. I was much more comfortable in adult situations most of the time. By seventh grade, I had finally figured out that it was much better to just be myself. When I quit trying so hard and was just me, I found other kids with similar interests.

Learning to get along with a lot of different people in life is a good skill but learning to be you is the most important lesson.

Be yourself. Be thankful you are not like anyone else. Not everyone will like you for who you are. You don't need everyone to like you and you don't need to like everyone else either. There are enough people in the world to go around for everybody.

EVERYONE CAN'T WIN

A lot of people, especially kids, believe that everyone is a winner because adults keep reinforcing that idea. The fact is, not everyone can win. It is not realistic. There will be winners and losers. Some people will not even say the word 'loser.' They think it is insulting. Just think how many times kids will tease calling each other 'loser.' If an adult is around, the next thing you hear is, "That's not nice. Don't call him a loser." Okay, I agree a little. Being called a loser is not the nicest word in the world but to take the complete opposite view and say that everyone is a winner is silly.

Think of a sport. You play all season and at the end, there are playoffs and then the tournaments. The purpose of the tournament is to see who the best team is overall. They become the winner. Depending on the league, the winning team gets an award or trophy or at a minimum, a certificate. Everyone else should just be happy with the experience and the fun of playing the sport. But should everyone get an award?

I played one season of flag football and one season of baseball when I was younger. My teams never won. All of the players still received trophies though. The coaches even made a point saying that they did not want to make anyone feel bad so they gave everyone something. It did not bother me that my team lost and I do not think we deserved a trophy just for playing. Another team won. They deserved the trophy.

People are too worried about hurting someone else's feelings. If a person realized that if they lose, they just have to try harder to earn the trophy. It would mean more in the long run.

If you know you do not have to try very hard and will still get rewarded, you will never really give it your all. Why should you? You know you will get something for nothing.

Schools reinforce this philosophy on a regular basis. Many times a teacher gives a good grade or extra credit whether the student put much effort in at all. It is almost as if teachers do not want to make students feel bad so they just give away grades instead of making kids earn them. Even though I try to do the best I can, it is hard to always give a hundred percent when I know I could save time, do a little less, and still get a good grade.

It has never made sense why people feel that they need to treat everyone exactly the same. When you get something just for participating instead of doing your best or reaching the goal, where is the incentive to try harder? I call this the *Just Breathing Award*. It seems like you do not even have to try very hard and you will still be rewarded. How does that teach anything in life?

Even the Academy Awards bought into the idea that no one is a loser. Way back when, after all the nominees were mentioned, they used to announce, "And the winner is. . ." That meant there was one winner and several losers. They eventually changed the wording to "And the award goes to. . . " Apparently no one wanted to think of themselves as the loser. I guess if no one says the word 'winner' people can ignore the fact that there is a loser also.

So what is the point? Life does not always have to make everyone happy with the outcome. Contests are not always fair. I try my best and if I win, that is great. If I lose, then I have learned that I need to try harder or do something different the next time if I want to win.

Let there be winners and let there be losers but everyone cannot win and it should be okay to say "you lost." How is anyone, especially a kid, supposed to learn how to deal with failing? Even the best motivational speakers say you need to fail sometimes in order to eventually succeed. Would successful business people be successful if they were handed everything without ever having to try? Do you get a bonus just for showing up for work every day?

My parents have taught me how important it is to try my best. They refuse to hand me things if I do not put the effort in myself. I have had my share of losing. Like most kids, I have been teased and called a loser at times for various reasons. Do I like it? Of course not. Is it reality? Sure. Tough times are supposed to make us work harder so we go from losing to winning.

IGNORE THE RULES

Wait! Calm down. This is not bad advice. I am not talking about breaking any laws or important rules. It is more like thinking outside the box and taking chances.

When I was eleven, we found a contest online from the Young Entrepreneurs of America. They were going to select a Young Entrepreneur of the Year. I got all excited thinking I had a good chance of winning. I read the requirements. My business fit all the criteria. I got even more excited. I knew I had just as much of a chance to win as anyone. As I read the rules, my excitement faded. I was too young. The rules stated that the contest was for kids sixteen and older. I guess they assumed that not many kids younger than that would have businesses.

I was already realizing the challenges of being a younger-than-average entrepreneur but I really wanted to win something like that. It was a huge award. I decided to enter anyway and ignore the rules.

In my entry form, I explained that there are kids much younger than sixteen who are doing amazing things in business. I went on to tell them about mine and suggested they consider me anyway. I figured that it was worth a try. What did I have to lose? Except for the award itself, it was just my time in filling out the form. And I could always say at least I tried.

Mom proofread everything. Then the big moment. CLICK. SUBMIT.

LIFE TIP: Don't let rules get in your way if you think you have something positive to offer.

I waited and waited and waited some more. It seemed like forever but it only took a few months until I received an email from the founder of the organization.

It said that the judges were so impressed with me, my business, and my charity work, but especially the fact that I entered the contest despite their age restrictions that they created a new category for Under 16. At eleven, I was the first recipient to win that award. That single contest is what really started the media ball rolling.

I am a rule follower by nature. I do not like getting in trouble. I try to do the right things. But I love telling that story especially if it can encourage other people to think outside the box. I look for opportunities like that any chance I get. There are not a lot of contests for entrepreneurs as young as I am. I have learned that if you want something, you need to go after it and sometimes that means ignoring the rules. The worst they can do is say no.

In 2009, I ran across a small business contest online sponsored by Intuit. The grand prize was a $25,000 business grant. Even the lesser prizes were pretty impressive. I was sure there was a minimum age requirement that I would not meet but we read the rules anyway. Sure enough, you had to be eighteen to enter. I thought I would try the same thing I had done with the Young Entrepreneur of the Year contest but this time I decided that I should probably get permission from someone first since my picture and story would be on

Intuit's website. Anyone that was of legal age that entered and saw my profile would wonder why I was there. I wanted to have an answer in case anyone questioned me.

Mom and I looked through the contest pages hoping to find an email address of someone connected to the contest. Our plan was to write them and ask permission to enter, realizing that they would not legally be able to award me anything. That was okay with me. I was going to be happy if they at least let me submit my story because it would be just one more website with free publicity for my business.

We could not find anyone's email address at Intuit connected with the contest. However, they did list the four judges, complete with names, pictures, and the company they worked for or owned. There was one man and three women. I chose the guy to send the email to hoping he might identify with me more if he had started his business when he was really young.

My email simply explained how old I was, what my business was, and that I was looking for someone at Intuit to contact about entering the contest. I asked if he could forward my email to the right person. Whenever I go out on a limb, I usually do not get too excited until I see results. The very next day, the judge emailed me saying how impressed he was with my business and the creativity that I showed in trying to enter the contest. He confirmed that he forwarded my email to an Intuit representative. That was good enough for me. At that point, it did not matter if it went any farther.

BIZ TIP: Sometimes the road getting there is more fun than reaching the end.

Things got more exciting. A day or two after his email, a woman from the contest contacted me. Her email gave me permission to submit my information online.

The contest deadline came and went and as expected, everybody that won was over eighteen. It was a good experience but the excitement wasn't over. Several weeks after the contest ended, I was notified that Intuit had started a special section called the Young Entrepreneur Movement. Each month they planned to feature young entrepreneurs and encourage other biz kids to join. I was excited to see that I was one of the first to be featured, no doubt because they were already aware of my business from their contest.

Being part of a global company's website was great but the surprises continued. Within a month after learning I was one of their first featured young entrepreneurs, I received a really surprising email from another Intuit employee. He told me that their corporate communications team was looking for stories that they could use for media and marketing purposes. He said that there was an opportunity with a reporter from *The New York Times* who was working on a story about teen entrepreneurs. He wanted my permission to forward my information to the reporter.

There were no guarantees that I would be interviewed with so many people to choose from but the fact that I had a possible opportunity with *The New York Times* was awesome!

I have had many opportunities from my business. Some of them I have initiated and sometimes reporters or producers have found me on their own. Either way, not every opportunity has become a reality but the experiences I have had along the way are more than I could have imagined.

Remember to try every possible opportunity. Breaking or ignoring the rules now and then may be just what pushes you to that next step.

THINGS ARE NOT ALWAYS WHAT THEY SEEM

The first time I was on national TV, I was a contestant on NBC's game show *1 vs 100*. One contestant competed against a mob of one hundred members. As each question was asked by host, Bob Saget, any contestant that answered correctly stayed in the game. If they answered incorrectly, they were eliminated. The amount of money increased with each question. The game was over when either the contestant eliminated all one hundred mob members and collected the jackpot or the contestant missed a question which meant the remaining mob members split whatever was in the jackpot at that time. The possible prize was a million dollars if anyone made it all the way.

For the episode I was in, the mob consisted of all kids competing against one adult. It was so much fun. There were Spelling Bee champions, Science Fair winners, a Jeopardy champion, and other special groups of kids. They had named me their 'kid mogul.' A mogul is a Bill Gates or Donald Trump. I was just a ten-year-old kid with a business but I liked the nickname they gave me anyway.

It was a long day. I experienced my first studio school because they had to provide a few teachers for all one hundred kids. But it was not like school at all. We took our own regular homework and an assigned teacher was simply there to monitor us and answer questions if necessary. I was so interested in everything else that was happening that I had a hard time concentrating on my work. Luckily, I had done most of my assignments the day before. I knew I would be too excited once I got there.

After several hours of waiting around with intermittent instructions about technical parts of the show and talking to certain kids, they finally took us into the studio taping area. One of the assistants marked my name badge with a code but did not tell me what it meant. I realized later once they had started taping the show.

As we walked in the studio, I wondered where the rest of the set was. Everything was so small and crammed together, nothing like it looked on television. There were a few sets of bleachers for the audience to sit on and tons of cords and electrical wires taped on the floor. The actual game set was pretty dull, literally. Until they turned on all of the lights, almost everything was black or gray. What a surprise that was. The colorful game sets you see on television are done with special effects and lighting.

Since they only allowed one parent to attend, Mom took me and Dad stayed home to work. As the kids were escorted into the game studio, the parents were taken into an empty adjoining studio where they watched the show on monitors. For many reasons, they had to keep us separated.

The one-hour long game show took several hours to tape. Sometimes the host would mess up on his lines or make jokes and they would have to re-do that part. At one point, they gave us a short bathroom break while they fixed technical problems. One of the things that they told us before we arrived was to wear comfortable shoes because we would be standing the whole time. They asked us to bring several different shirts for them to approve but did not care what bottoms we wore since each person's counter would hide them from the waist down.

We had no idea what the actual questions were before the show started. Even though the mob was all kids, the questions were not kid specific. The first question was easy. It referred to a Wii. I did not have one but I definitely knew what a Wii was. One girl missed that question. We all felt sorry for her because that meant she was out of the game. We also wondered how any kid could miss that question since it was probably the most popular game system out that year. The light in her box went dark and that was the last we saw of her.

One down. Ninety-nine to go. None of us knew how many more questions we would be faced with. The second question was a bit more confusing. *If Heathcliff the cat lived kitty-corner to Garfield, where would his house be in relation to Garfield's?* Mom used the term 'kitty-corner' all the time. I knew it meant diagonally but for whatever reason, I did not pick the right answer. Thank goodness I was not the only one who got the answer wrong. Forty-four other kids also missed that question. Now it was my turn to sit in a dark box for the rest of the show. All I could think of was how fast my time on TV went.

Oh wait, it wasn't over.

The audience sighed. It was obvious they felt bad for the kids that were eliminated. I was expecting my box to go dark right away along with all of the other kids that missed the question, but Bob Saget decided to talk with me. Yes, that's right, on camera! How much better free publicity could I get for my business than on national TV? My heart was beating really fast. I was nervous I would mess up. When I realized the camera was on me, I took a deep breath and smiled.

"We lost our kid mogul," Bob said. "Tell us your name." So I did. He asked what made me a kid mogul. I was pretty nervous so I was talking faster than normal. Apparently, he did not understand that I said Pencil Bugs (plural) so I corrected him waving my hand in an 'S' motion in the air and repeating Bugs with an 'S'. The audience laughed. The kids laughed. The contestant laughed. The host laughed. I nervously laughed. Then Bob made a joke about it and more laughter continued while he asked me a few more questions. I loved being in the spotlight. At that moment, I did not care at all that I was eliminated and missed a chance at the money. I knew my time on national television was going to mean more in the long run.

After our short conversation, the light went out in my box along with the other kids that missed that question and they continued with the game. In the end, the contestant missed a question which made the remaining five kids in the mob split $94,000.

That day was so fun. Oh sure, it would have been nice to win some of the money and make it to the end but I did not go into it expecting to win anything. What I got out of it was worth so much more.

The next day it was back to school as usual and being a normal kid again. My website was flooded with orders for Pencil Bugs. People were sending emails with congratulations even though I did not win which I thought was really nice of them to do. However, not all of the messages were polite. Even though I was only in the spotlight for a few minutes, it was my first experience with people who were obviously anxious to make negative comments.

While I was in school, Mom checked messages and printed out product orders. When she saw the first nasty email, she wondered whether or not to tell me. The message was pointless and not worth repeating. It was clear that the person had way too much time on their hands and was mad at the whole world. I just happened to be what he was watching on his television that night.

By the time Mom picked me up from school, she had decided that it was better that I learn how to deal with negative people right then and there. Since my business was relatively new, we were not sure how big it would become. In the event that I continued to get more publicity, she knew that there was always a chance that other people would make senseless comments at some point. She showed me the email. I did not know the guy who wrote it so I did not give it too much thought.

The next day, I received another email from a woman who also watched the show. Her comments were specific to the way I acted. She thought I was rude to the host by the way I corrected my business name and talked really slowly to make sure he understood me the second time I said it. She was not aware that the producer gave the kids instructions before the taping to have fun, make jokes, give the host information that he could make jokes about and be excited. I was not planning on saying or doing what I did but it worked. The audience laughed and had a good time. Afterward, the production people said I was very entertaining. That is the point of most television shows -- entertainment.

Normally, Mom would not have taken the time to respond to negative emails but because this particular one attacked my behavior, she felt the need to send an email back explaining the producer's instructions to the kids. Surprisingly, we received another email from the woman apologizing for not realizing what went on behind the scenes.

Things are not always what they seem. I thought the studio would be more elaborate. I had no idea it took hours to make a one-hour show. And viewers are not always aware of off-camera instructions.

Now that you know who won the money, I can let you in on a funny little secret. One of the technical problems happened right at the moment the contestant missed his question. As Bob Saget announced that the contestant lost and the remaining kids in the mob won, the contestant had an obvious look of disappointment. He just lost $94,000. As the audience clapped and the camera panned around the five kids who won, they made an announcement that they had to tape that part over. The poor guy had to go through losing again and make it look like he was genuinely surprised and disappointed all over again. Whatever the technical difficulties were, they needed a third retake so he had to go back on stage and lose one more time. I was glad I was not him at that moment. Missing the second question was not half as bad as what he was going through. Of course, what ended up on television was all edited and no one knew the difference except all of us who were in the studio that day.

All of the contestants were required to sign a release and confidentiality form before the show. No one was allowed to say who won until the show finally aired which was not until a few weeks later. The five kids who won probably had the toughest time. They each had just won $18,800 and could not tell a single soul.

Things are not always what they seem. Sometimes they are actually much more fun!

IT COSTS NOTHING TO BE POLITE

By the way some people act, you would think it was the hardest thing in the world for them to be nice to another person.

Everyone has probably heard at one point, "If you can't say anything nice, don't say anything at all." I know I have heard it more than a few times myself. We all say mean things once in awhile. We are only human.

Sometimes it is pretty hard to be nice. When you are in an argument with someone, being nice is the farthest thing from your mind. Not only is it hard to be nice but it is even harder to keep quiet. Out it comes. A nasty remark. If it did not cause the argument to get worse, at a minimum it made the other person feel bad.

Within a split second, you wish you could take it back. Reverse time. Get a do-over. But that never happens. That is the bad part of speaking before you think and letting your frustrations or other emotions speak for you.

When I first started playing golf with my dad, I could usually convince him to let me have a certain amount of mulligans. They are great. You make a mistake, hit a bad shot, and you do not have to count that stroke. It is as if it never even happened at all. Unfortunately, that does not work with words. Once you say something, it is out there forever.

LIFE TIP: There are no mulligans once words come out of your mouth.

When kids are really young, they usually say whatever is on their minds. At that age, most people think kids are being cute so their outbursts are overlooked. As we grow up, we are supposed to know what is appropriate.

The next time you are in a situation where you might say something nasty, wait ten seconds. That might be all it takes to avoid wishing you could have the do-over, reverse time, or take it all back.

OFFER A SOLUTION, NOT A COMPLAINT

Everyone can probably think of at least a few people they know who are complainers. They just love to complain. They complain about everything and anything, any chance they get.

Kids are usually good at complaining because, for the most part, the world revolves around them, or at least many think it does.

I will admit, there have been times when my parents have had to remind me that the world does not revolve around me. Whoa! What a surprise that was. When I was much younger, my typical response was, "What? Yes, it does!"

I have done my fair share of complaining. It is hard for kids to think things through to the next step in order to offer a solution to the problem that they are complaining about. Learning the best way to handle different situations is an ongoing process. Sometimes offering a solution to a problem works and things improve. Sometimes it doesn't. At least people know you are not just there to complain. You have something of value to offer also.

It takes a lot of energy to constantly complain and what does it get you? If you do it too much, people may start to avoid you. Then if you actually have something of value to add or suggest, you could be ignored. If I get on a roll where I complain too much about something, Mom and Dad just tune me out. I finally get the point and realize my way will not get me very far.

Complaining without offering a solution does not accomplish much. However, a situation cannot change or improve if people keep quiet. Speaking up and voicing your opinion is really important. It is how you communicate it that makes the difference.

Three Things to Make a Difference in the World

Since I was old enough to talk, I have been included in a lot of adult conversations with my family but also with other grown-ups. A lot of that probably has to do with being an only child. It seems we are a different type of kid and learn more about life and adult things sooner than most other kids do. I am not saying that is good or bad. It is just the way it seems to be.

I have barely just begun. I have my whole life ahead of me. Once in awhile, I wonder how I will be remembered after I am gone. I have also asked my parents what they think my purpose is while I am here. They tell me that I do not have to worry about that. They also remind me of all the good things that I am doing to help other kids through my donations and how I encourage people to try their ideas and to be positive.

Many people go through life never knowing what their purpose is. I guess that is probably the way it is meant to be. If we knew why we were on earth, maybe we would not like the reason. Sometimes you just have to believe without knowing.

LIFE TIP: Everyone can make a difference in the world.

A few years ago, my parents and I were at a restaurant. While we were waiting for our food to come, I was making notes for this book. A guy at the next table said to me, "You shouldn't work so hard." I told him I was not working. I was writing my first book.

He chuckled, probably because he was not expecting that answer from a kid. I could see his point. Writing a book was kind of odd when you think of how many kids play hand-held games or text or are on a cell phone in a public place. You do not really expect them to be working.

We talked for awhile and then he told me that there are three things a person should do to leave their mark on the world.

1. Raise a child.
2. Plant a tree.
3. Write a book.

"Well," I said. "Obviously, I have not raised a child yet but I will probably get married some day and have kids. Just last year, I helped my parents plant a lemon tree in our back yard. And about writing the book? Well, I guess I will have that one covered pretty soon."

Two out of three isn't bad, especially for someone my age. When you think of it, those three things are great to leave for the future and hopefully they will improve it in some way.

Since Grandma had written her book, had raised five kids and had planted many, many trees on their ranch, I wanted to see if she had ever heard the same thing that guy told me. No surprise. Of course she had heard something similar before. She agreed that was pretty important and reminded me that accomplishing those three things are easier than most people think.

"First of all," she said. "Raising a child does not mean you actually have to have one or be a parent.

There are many ways to help raise a child especially with so many extended families today. Second, even if a person lives in an apartment without any space to plant a tree, something as simple as donating one to an organization to plant it for you is just as helpful."

As I listened to Grandma, I was pretty sure I knew where she was going with this. I had heard Mom and Grandma talk for hours on the phone when they were working on Grandma's book. Grandma always thought it was important to have things written down on paper and print out photos because so many people only have things on their computers or CDs.

"And about writing a book," Grandma continued. "It isn't that critical to get the book published. It is more important to have the words down on paper even if you just make one copy for yourself. As long as someone else knows where it is, at least they will be able to pass it down to the next generation."

I have a lot of very wise people in my life. You probably do too. No matter how young or old you are, everyone can make a difference in the world. It takes action, effort, and persistence. Even if you wonder why you are here, just believe there is a reason and accept that you may never know. Try to make a difference for the next generation.

KEEPING BALANCED

You can have it all. At least that is what many people think, especially kids. We want it all. We want it now. And we want it all now! The truth is, anyone can have it all, just not all at the same time.

Regardless of your age, family, work or school situation, if you think you have it all, you are probably missing something. There are only so many hours in a day. Even for me on a typical school day, I wish that I had more time to play after I get homework done. If I played first and then did my homework last, it would probably take me a lot longer to get it done because I would be more tired at the end of the night. I would be going to bed later than usual which would mean I would get less sleep. That would cause me to be more tired the next day at school. It is a snowball effect. Having it all and all at the same time is usually too good to be true.

LIFE TIP: Something always has to give.

One of the most frequent questions I get asked is how I manage everything. What is my secret to keeping the balance between being a kid, going to school, having friends, and also having my business?

The key to my balancing act is my parents. Even before I started my business, they never believed in over-scheduling me with extracurricular activities. In early elementary school, I liked singing so I performed in several talent shows. Later I wanted to try team sports. My parents let me choose one sport at a time to see which one I liked the best. It turned out after several seasons of different sports that I really did not like any of them that much. I did, however, take Tae Kwon Do for four years but most of that was before my business got going.

I was never so busy that we were running from one practice to the next, eating fast food on the go, doing homework late into the night, and getting little sleep. Nope. My parents thought that there were better ways to spend a childhood.

I looked at some of my friends and all of the extra things that they were doing and wondered when they ever had time to just be a regular kid and play or even be bored once in awhile. Some of them did not even have a concept of being bored which I thought was pretty sad because that meant they were always on the go. It is good to be bored once in awhile. You might be surprised at how creative you can be when you have free time and are not rushing to get somewhere. I have had some of my best ideas when I have been bored.

No matter what age you are, no one can have it all. If you really look at the situation, there will be consequences somewhere. It may be as simple as not having as much free time to just do nothing. Or it may be that there is not enough time spent with family or friends. Or a kid's grades go down because there is not enough time for homework and studying. Or a person gains weight because they are always eating junk food on the run. You are kidding yourself if you think that you can have it all and all at the same time.

LIFE TIP: Being balanced is more important than trying to have it all.

I am lucky that I still have all of my grandparents as well as many other older relatives. When you ask an older person if they would change anything about their life, they typically do not say they wished that they would have worked more. They usually say that they wished they had spent more time with their family and friends.

My advice to parents would be to not over-schedule your kids. They may not tell you exactly how they feel but I bet deep down, they would rather be spending time with you and friends or even just having more free time. They can always cram in all the extracurricular activities they want when they are older but they cannot get their childhood back. We only have one chance at that. Running from one activity to another, eating on the run, not having any time to stop and take a breath may not be the best in the long run.

How do I keep balanced? School comes first, then being a normal kid, and then my business. Do I think I have it all now? Definitely not. I wouldn't want to. I have a whole lifetime ahead of me and plenty of time to have it all, just not all at the same time.

Jason O'Neill

TEXTBOOKS FOR SCHOOL – PRACTICAL EXPERIENCE AND COMMON SENSE FOR LIFE

Before teachers and principals get all crazy reading this, I have always liked school and I am an A-student. But as I have gotten older, it seems like we waste more and more time in school, especially on information that does not really prepare us for the real world or have practical value. I am sure every person who has gone to school has felt this way at one time or another.

LIFE TIP: Real life is an education.

As my business has grown, I have had so many experiences and opportunities that have shown me what the real world is like. Typical educators and entrepreneurs are usually on opposite sides of the fence. In my experience, I have not found many people in education that even understand entrepreneurship. Even in private schools, education is pretty basic. Why should they teach anything about entrepreneurship or how to be self-sufficient? School is about textbooks, tests, grades, and diplomas. They tell us that they are preparing us for college. That is supposed to lead to getting a degree and eventually finding an eight-to-five job with a company. If you are lucky, you are smart and will pick a field or degree that will be in demand. Otherwise, you will end up like so many people have today where their degree gets them nothing. Traditional schools forget about the possibilities and opportunities of becoming an entrepreneur.

Math has always been my favorite subject. Part of the reason may be because I have always had an interest in money, saving, and investing. I remember asking my dad at a really young age how the stock market worked. When I entered sixth grade, I was bumped up to seventh grade math. It was fun. I was learning a lot of new concepts, although it was hard to see how some of them would have practical applications in the real world.

One day as I was balancing my bank statement for Pencil Bugs, Mom stopped me. "Have any of your math teachers ever taught the kids how to balance a checkbook?" Mom had always been really involved at my schools helping the teachers on many projects. Neither one of us could remember anyone teaching that skill.

Balancing a checkbook is not that difficult because it is simple addition and subtraction. But if a person has never even seen the layout of a check register or seen a bank statement, it would be confusing the first time. It would make sense that in some math class along the way, a teacher would have used a checkbook to show how math relates to the real world.

There are so many times where real-life applications could be integrated into the classroom, making it more interesting and relevant for students. Education is not only about textbooks, memorizing, tests, grades, and the degree.

LIFE TIP: Learn it. Don't just memorize it.

Most kids hate memorizing things, especially when you wonder when you will ever need to know it in real life. Think of the things you had to memorize in school. How many of them can you still recite today or how often do you really need to?

For most people, memorizing is short term. As soon as we take the test or recite the speech, it leaves our memory banks. We have to make room for more information, more things to memorize. Wouldn't it be better if a person learned where to go to look up the information rather than trying to memorize a lot of things that they will probably never need in their normal everyday life?

School is great for teaching textbook information. Look for other opportunities to learn about real life. When I give talks at schools about my business, I tell the students that school should come first as it still does with me. However, I also let them know about all of the things that I have learned from having my business. Sometimes it is tough to balance school and business but the opportunities and experiences I have had are well worth the effort.

I know there are certain requirements that schools have to follow in order to get students through high school. Just think of the possibilities though if entrepreneurship, common sense, and practical applications were included in education.

CONCLUSION

So many people make things harder than they need to be. That does not mean you will never run into challenges. What matters most is how you look at things. More often than not, it just takes common sense.

Life can be fun. Remember to make time for what matters. Time is the one thing that you can never get back or do over. Just because you grow up, you can still be a kid at heart. There is a huge difference between being child-like and child-ish.

Business can be fun too. It can teach you more than you ever imagined. If you start your own business, the things that you will learn about yourself, other people, and life in general will amaze you. Be open to all possibilities. Believe in yourself but ask for help when you need it. No one can do this alone.

Whenever you find yourself wondering how you will accomplish something, remember to simplify things. Look at the big picture but take tiny steps one at a time. Before long, you will have reached your goal and the journey may be more fun than the end result.

BIZ TIP: Try your ideas!

WHAT'S NEXT?

I do not have all of the answers. I don't pretend to. If I ever start acting like I know everything, my parents are right there to set me straight.

What I do know is that I plan on learning as much as I can, listening to people who know more than I do, and helping people of all ages as much as possible along the way.

With the help of my parents, I am working hard to make Pencil Bugs into the mega empire that I envision. When I was ten years old, I received a Young Philanthropist Award for my donations to help other kids. I hope to make enough money in the future with my business to help thousands of kids all over the world.

But if for some unforeseen reason my plans do not turn out as expected, I will still go on to do great things. And I will always look back on this time and have great memories of the amazing opportunities and fun experiences that I had because I was "the Pencil Bugs kid."

45 TIPS FOR BUSINESS AND LIFE

BIZ TIP: Don't pick the first business or product name you think of. Give it a lot of thought. It will be harder and more costly later on to change your mind. (10)

BIZ TIP: Looking back is easy. Making changes today is what matters. (17)

BIZ TIP: An idea is just a thought unless you act on it. (18)

LIFE TIP: Doing nothing will guarantee nothing. (20)

BIZ TIP: From the moment you get an idea, start keeping a journal. (21)

LIFE TIP: Be patient. Don't give up! (27)

BIZ TIP: You have to make things happen but don't force things to happen. (27)

LIFE TIP: It is okay to ask for help. (28)

BIZ TIP: Money is good to have but it is more important what you do with it once you have it. (31)

LIFE TIP: Treat people with respect because every person matters. (39)

BIZ TIP: Without customers, you have no business. (41)

BIZ TIP: Less of a good thing is better than more of a bad thing. (43)

BIZ TIP: A website does not mean you are going to see instant success or sales. (45)

BIZ TIP: The only bad idea is no idea. (47)

BIZ TIP: Develop friendships not just business connections. (56)

LIFE TIP: Everyone deserves to be acknowledged and recognized. (59)

LIFE TIP: Don't limit your opportunities. (61)

LIFE TIP: Older people can learn from someone much younger too. (63)

BIZ TIP: Wealth is simply a perception. (72)

BIZ TIP: If you do anything in life strictly for the money, you are doing it for the wrong reasons. (74)

BIZ TIP: Public speaking is like having a conversation in your living room but with a much larger group of people. (78)

LIFE TIP: Remember, everyone makes mistakes. (82)

LIFE TIP: If you make a mistake, get over it and move on. (95)

LIFE TIP: The worse mistake is one that you don't learn from. (97)

LIFE TIP: Having fun is not just for kids. (101)

LIFE TIP: A nervous smile is always better than no smile. (103)

BIZ TIP: Don't assume your plan will work every time. (106)

LIFE TIP: The easiest way to be ready for anything is not to procrastinate. (111)

LIFE TIP: Be practical and use common sense. Not everything is written in a textbook. (121)

BIZ TIP: Sometimes the perfect job doesn't exist until you create it yourself. (123)

BIZ TIP: Be financially smart. Don't quit your current job until you find a new one. (124)

LIFE TIP: Stand up for what you believe in even if you are the only one standing. (128)

BIZ TIP: Keep going even if you want to quit sometimes. (132)

LIFE TIP: Remember the big picture when you get tired of the small day-to-day things. (135)

LIFE TIP: Keep it in perspective. Don't overdo it. (140)

LIFE TIP: Like yourself for who you are. (143)

LIFE TIP: Don't let rules get in your way if you think you have something positive to offer. (149)

BIZ TIP: Sometimes the road getting there is more fun than reaching the end. (151)

LIFE TIP: There are no mulligans once words come out of your mouth. (160)

LIFE TIP: Everyone can make a difference in the world. (164)

LIFE TIP: Something always has to give. (167)

LIFE TIP: Being balanced is more important than trying to have it all. (169)

LIFE TIP: Real life is an education. (170)

LIFE TIP: Learn it. Don't just memorize it. (171)

BIZ TIP: Try your ideas! (173)

ABOUT THE AUTHOR

Entrepreneur Jason O'Neill is a regular teenager who saw an opportunity at the age of nine to make some money. He took action and Pencil Bugs were quickly born. Little did he know that the simple idea he created for a craft fair would become a successful business earning him awards and national media acclaim. Jason was the youngest person at age eleven to receive the Young Entrepreneur of the Year Award and was named to a *Forbes* Top 10 List of Role Models 18 and Under at age twelve.

Jason speaks at schools (elementary through college), libraries, businesses, organizations, and conferences encouraging and inspiring people of all ages to try their ideas and give back to their communities. He donates a portion of his proceeds to help other kids and one day hopes to become a worldwide philanthropist.

Jason lives with his parents and dog, Rusty, in southern California. He enjoys family vacations, golfing with his dad, swimming, playing with his friends, and of course, playing video games. In addition to continuing to expand his Pencil Bugs business and publish his children's books featuring the Pencil Bugs characters, Jason has aspirations to be a video game designer.

For more information about Jason O'Neill or Pencil Bugs, please visit *www.pencilbugs.com*.

CPSIA information can be obtained at www.ICGtesting.com
Printed in the USA
LVOW01s1451011113

359624LV00018B/524/P